HOW TO STUDY THE BEHAVIOR OF CHILDREN

by

Gertrude Driscoll, Ph.D.

Associate Professor of Education
Teachers College, Columbia University

BUREAU OF PUBLICATIONS

TEACHERS COLLEGE : COLUMBIA UNIVERSITY

NEW YORK

PRINTED IN THE UNITED STATES OF AMERICA
BY NEW YORK LITHOGRAPHING CORPORATION

Editor's Introduction

BEHAVIOR problems have always been one of the major concerns of teachers. Historically, most teachers viewed these problems as the troublesome aspects of teaching which somehow or other must be "handled" in order that the work of the school might go forward. The young teacher was fearful of not being able to handle *discipline*, of not having the knack of making pupils "behave." The experienced teacher's success was evaluated to no small degree in terms of classroom order. Generally, these problems were viewed as more or less incidental to the teaching role of the teacher.

In modern practices an entirely different view has developed. The general area of behavior is recognized as one of the important responsibilities of education in which teachers should work with as much expertness and knowledge as in the more conventional aspects of the school program. Behavior problems do not arise from innate "orneryness." They reflect important aspects of the developing child's personality and must be understood by teachers in this larger relationship if schools are to educate in any complete sense of the term. Teachers should learn to detect a child's behavior problems which do not result in group conflict or departure from customary rules of conduct as well as the more obvious ones.

These responsibilities for understanding behavior and guiding children in the development of satisfactory relationships with others are difficult for many teachers to discharge because teacher education has generally given relatively little attention to behavior problems. Much needs to be done in strengthening this aspect of teacher education both on the pre-service and in-service levels. This monograph will give direct help to teachers on the practical problems of behavior. It will be found valuable by the teacher in the field facing children day after day and

▾

by the teacher in training. It is *down to earth* in that it provides suggestions which the regular classroom teacher can follow without an elaborate guidance organization or the extensive assistance of specialists. The material is designed for the classroom teacher, supervisor, and principal, taking its setting from the usual classroom situation.

H. L. CASWELL
Professor of Education and
Director of Division and Instruction
Teachers College
Columbia University

Contents

HOW TO STUDY
THE BEHAVIOR OF
CHILDREN

CHAPTER ONE

Opportunities for Studying Children's Behavior

TEACHERS in the elementary grades have unparalleled opportunities to study human behavior. The extent to which each teacher is able to make use of this opportunity depends on her training, experience, and insight. The teacher whose training has made her aware of the complex nature of behavior sees each child as an individual. She seeks to interpret his behavior through an understanding of growth processes and conditions which have contributed to make him the kind of person he is. In the light of her understanding and insight she formulates for each individual child a plan which is designed to develop his potentialities for growth. For her, experience with children is not mere routine but a creative opportunity.

Our first task is to survey the school situation to see what opportunities are offered for the study of children's behavior. In order to comprehend the full range of each child's personality it is essential to study his behavior in a variety of situations, to study his responses to experiences in his everyday life both in school and out of school.

Opportunities for studying children's behavior are provided in three areas: First, in the *classroom*, where individuals strive through varied experiences to live cooperatively with one another, to maintain individuality of the self, and to acquire those tools and knowledges considered essential by our culture. Second, on the *playground*, where physical processes and efficiency play a leading role. Third, through *out-of-school* activities, where differences in cultural pressures may be observed. Information obtained from these sources may be supplemented by additional facts gained from parents regarding their children's growth.

The study of children's behavior is pertinent for all teachers and particularly for the teacher of the elementary grades. At one time it was believed that the purpose of education was to train the mind. Now educators are accepting the fact that education must encourage growth in all areas of development. Educators who are interested primarily in academic achievements are realizing more clearly that they are not successful in obtaining the intellectual growth desired when other aspects of growth are ignored. Intellect is a part of the whole organism; it does not function alone. To obtain satisfactory intellectual achievement, we must have a physically healthy child who is accepted in his own social group. Disturbances in physical, social, or emotional health limit ability to concentrate, to memorize, to reason logically, or to respond to classroom stimulation. Thus, all aspects of growth must be considered in order to accomplish the traditional goal of education—intellectual development and academic achievement. Educators are becoming interested in all aspects of growth because they realize that the individual as a functioning unit in society is basically the primary goal of education. In a cooperative society, individuals must be prepared to contribute to the community. Skills are essential, but unless they can be used to work with one's peers they are of little value. Development of the individual as a contributing member of society demands that we educate in all areas of growth. To work more intelligently toward this goal requires a fundamental understanding of children's behavior.

In this chapter the teacher's opportunities for child study are discussed at length. The following chapter presents various methods that the teacher may use in gaining greater understanding of behavior. In the final chapter suggestions are offered to the teacher for utilizing the knowledge gained of children's behavior for the guidance of individual children in a classroom situation.

THE CLASSROOM

A classroom that offers a variety of activities stimulates a broad range of responses. As soon as formal subject matter loosens its stranglehold upon the daily program, other types of work may be undertaken. Even though academic experiences still predominate, a change in approach, based on children's interests, will bring true personality patterns into action. The receptive automaton vanishes. We are faced with children who differ from one another; we find that the approach and response of each have distinct characteristics. When academic experiences become the vehicle for growth rather than ends in themselves, still further opportunity is offered for variety of responses. This is particularly true if spontaneous expression is encouraged through dramatics, composition, music, fine arts, and industrial arts. To the extent that we challenge interests and allow expression of them, we change the classroom from a situation in which children are molded in one cast to a situation in which feeling, acting, expressive children live each day.

Classroom activities may include four general types of experiences:

1. Experiences in skill subjects, including reading, arithmetic, writing, spelling, social studies, composition.
2. Experiences in working with others in a group, such as planning activities, discussion, joint activities in a unit of work, preparing and serving lunch, planning and taking excursions.
3. Aesthetic experiences, including music, poetry, art.
4. Creative experiences in dramatics, rhythm, color and form, plastic materials, wood-block printing, science.

Children seldom exhibit the same kind of behavior in each of these activities. It is important to determine the variations in behavior which may be expected among a normal class of thirty-five children.

BEHAVIOR RESPONSE TO SKILL SUBJECTS

Skill subjects, though they differ markedly in content, make many common demands upon children. They require a high degree of attention when explanations of principles or procedure are being given by the teacher; preparation of a plan of work or following a plan set by the teacher; persistence in carrying through a plan to completion. What lies behind the responses that children make to these requirements?

Various conditions affect the degree of attention that children are able to give to the teacher's explanation.

1. The experiences that the child has had between the time he left school the previous day and his return to school in the morning may affect his degree of attention.

The Case of James

James, in the fourth grade, never knew what to expect when he returned home from school. Sometimes his mother was happy to see him. After a brief greeting he would be allowed to go out to play. At other times his mother would scold him the minute he entered the house. Everything would be topsy-turvy in the house because his mother had had one of her "streaks" of running around and upsetting things. On the day after finding his mother this way he kept wondering how things would be when he got home, and he would often miss some of the explanation that the teacher was giving.

2. When a child is suffering personal discomfort he naturally is aware of the discomfort and "pays attention" to it. This discomfort may be either emotional, physical, or social in character.

The Case of ~~Jane~~ Abbie Jorgenson

Jane had frequently been told that she was a "queer" child. Her mother had said she had better change or she would have no friends. In the classroom she sat next to a girl who seemed to think that she was "funny." When the teacher was giving an explanation Jane would often wonder what that girl thought of her. She would find herself looking hard at the girl, trying to read her thoughts and before she knew it she had missed an important explanation that the teacher was giving.

3. An unfortunate earlier experience with the subject under

discussion frequently causes a child to feel such apprehension whenever the subject is broached that thinking becomes confused and attention wavers.

The Case of ~~Nancy~~ Helen Hallovan

Nancy could never forget the terrible time her "friend" Mary had last year when she was unable to get an arithmetic problem. The teacher would not believe that Mary could not get the answer to the problem. Mary wept and the teacher scolded. Up to that time Nancy had been able to understand arithmetic but she had always thought that Mary was better in arithmetic than she was. Every time they had arithmetic she tried to become inconspicuous so that she would escape the notice of the teacher. She was so occupied with making herself as inconspicuous as possible that she found she was missing a great deal that the teacher explained.

4. Many children have learned from previous experience that adults repeat remarks and directions many times. They have formed the habit of attending only when the tone of voice indicates that attention is necessary.

The Case of John

John's mother talked a great deal. During the day when he was the only person around she talked so much to him that he could not keep his mind on the things that he was doing. He found that he could ignore what his mother was saying unless her voice became sharp. In the first grade his teacher had a very quiet voice. There were many materials around the room that interested him. He was not aware of the fact that the teacher frequently gave him special directions. Because of the consideration shown him he arrived in the second grade still paying no attention to general directions.

EFFECT OF APTITUDE UPON RESPONSE
TO A PARTICULAR SUBJECT

Children are acutely aware of their special aptitudes and also their limitations in a particular subject. When attacking a task in which they have special aptitude their behavior response is direct, confident, ingenious. They are able to show versatility and freedom in their work because of the mastery they have of fundamental techniques. On the other hand, recognized limitation in a subject causes behavior to be restricted, cautious, often blundering. Ice skating, for example, reveals dramatically the difference between aptitude in a skill and limitation. The skilled performer moves with grace and freedom, experiments confidently with new figures. The novice moves awkwardly and with caution, gives evidence of his temerity with every step.

Aptitude may be affected by inability to comprehend the subject, inadequate foundation in the subject, and conditioning against the subject.

Inability to comprehend the subject. In schools where subject matter is determined by grade level rather than children's development, many children are exposed to ideas that they are unable to comprehend. They are defeated before they attempt to attack the work. These children frequently are described as "lazy," "inattentive," "indifferent." What ability they may possess is dulled by the inevitability of failure.

Inadequate foundation in the subject. Children frequently are shifted from one school to another. They enter a grade on the basis of previous subject matter studied. Yet no two teachers cover similar subject matter in the same way. In such sequential subjects as arithmetic and spelling, shifts in schools, absences, and variability of teachers may prevent children from acquiring the fundamental learnings essential to intelligent pursuit of the work.

Conditioning against the subject. In family groups attitudes regarding particular subject matter are freely expressed. Parents recall difficulties they experienced in school. Older brothers and sisters conjure the vicissitudes they suffered in a particular subject. By the time some children gain their initial experience in reading, arithmetic, or spelling they have built up a picture of difficulty that they feel certain is beyond their level of ability.

SIGNIFICANCE OF WORK HABITS

Work habits include the approach children make to a task to be done, whether the task is one set by the teacher or by themselves. Some children may vary their work habits, showing excellent planning and execution when they are interested in a task and working much less efficiently when they are not interested. Many children, however, are quite consistent in the work habit pattern they use.

Work habits are affected by several factors: teacher approval, confidence in one's own ability, difference in temperament, physical well-being.

Teacher approval. All children who feel they have a chance to secure approval of the teacher will work for that approval. School is competitive not only in academic achievement but also in securing teacher approval. The way children attack their work is often conditioned by teacher approval.

Confidence in own ability. The confidence that a child feels in his ability to do his work has a direct effect on his approach to it. Haphazard approach, trial and error in getting started, innumerable emergencies, such as losing pencils, eraser, or some other necessary equipment, indicate that he is uncertain how to move toward the work at hand. Step by step directions may help in clarifying his procedure.

Difference in temperament. Some children accept specific directions, feeling much more comfortable when they know exactly what is to be done and just how to do it. Other children accept the task more readily if they are allowed to work out their own plans. An alert teacher will notice these differences in temperament in the work response of her pupils.

Physical well-being. Healthy children are energetic children. Children who feel chronic fatigue, who are malnourished, or who are subject to eye-strain, frequent colds, or other physical disabilities have less energy at their disposal. They become discouraged easily. The teacher should look for physical causes behind laziness, lack of persistence, irritability, or general passivity.

BEHAVIOR RESPONSES WHEN WORKING WITH OTHERS IN A GROUP

All group activities require that individuality be curbed to some extent and that group interests be considered by all. For many children, and even some adults, group cooperation is difficult. Normally, children in the upper elementary school begin to desire to be part of the group to the extent of foregoing some individual interest. The degree of interest in an activity, the extent to which the group wishes to follow their individual interests, and the length of time they are required to follow group wishes determine their success in maintaining a cooperative attitude. Through observation of children in group activity and in individual activity, the teacher may gauge their readiness for cooperative activity.

Among the factors that affect ability to cooperate with others are degree of cooperation required, social relationship, opportunity for leadership, and self-confidence.

Degree of cooperation required. Many children begin an activity with zest. Five or ten minutes pass in cooperative work, and then a disagreement arises. Upon inquiry the teacher finds that the erstwhile enthusiast is unable to accept the plan of work agreed upon by the others. More cooperation has been required than he is emotionally or socially able to give.

Social relationships. Comfortable social relationships affect responses in group work. Children usually work smoothly with a group in which they have friends. Put these children in groups where friends are lacking and their ability to work with others decreases.

Opportunity for leadership. Real leadership requires the ability to cooperate with a group. Frequently, leaders accept cooperation as a necessity if the advantages of leadership are to be retained. The teacher may observe marked individual differences in children's ability to cooperate with others by noting cooperation given under leadership conditions and under non-leadership conditions.

Self-confidence. Highly egocentric children have difficulty in becoming submerged in a group relationship. Highly egocentric behavior indicates that the individual lacks confidence. To move forward in cooperative behavior these children must feel sure enough of themselves to be willing to remain unnoticed. The teacher should be aware of the children in her classroom who are too insecure to be successful in group cooperation.

RESPONSE TO AESTHETIC EXPERIENCE

Response to the aesthetic may be both intellectual and emotional. For full appreciation of the aesthetic a feeling response is required. Tones of music, for example, may be high or low tones to some children; they may be warm, intense, or soothing to others. Every child has the potential ability to respond with feeling to aesthetic experiences. The difference in response that children make to experiences of color, form, musical tones, melodies, and poetry tells us a great deal about them.

Tense, inhibited children are often fearful of letting themselves respond to aesthetic experiences. As a general rule, inhibited children try to ignore their feelings by tightening control over them. They feel so deeply that they are afraid to give their emotions expression. These children frequently are restricted in speech, awkward in movement, and unable to respond to the full measure of their ability.

Group responses to the aesthetic tend to emphasize understanding or reasoned responses to the experience. Description and explanations of the meaning conveyed in a poem, picture, or song are primarily intellectual responses. Emotional responses are conveyed through selection by individuals of the part of the experience most pleasing to them, of individual expression of the mood conveyed through other media, such as rhythm, dramatics, plastic or fine arts, or through enjoyment in repeating the experience. Children who show only a passing interest in an aesthetic experience are responding intellectually and therefore do not fully appreciate the emotional nuances and moods portrayed.

Emotional responses require a comfortable social relationship. The teacher who encourages individuality in her classroom will find children responding spontaneously to aesthetic experiences. Although emotional responses are individual, a relaxed friendly relationship between teacher and pupil sets the stage for natural emotional appreciation of the aesthetic. The teacher should strive for social relationships which encourage spontaneous class appreciation of music, poetry, form, or color.

CREATIVE EXPRESSION

Creative expression requires freedom in the medium of expression and skill enough to carry out the desired idea on a level satisfying to the individual. Frequently to the layman the creative expression of children in the primary grades appears crude, unimaginative, and lacking in educational value. In order to convince the lay public that work in color, clay, or dramatics is educational, emphasis often is placed on skill in these areas rather than on creativity. When this is done, the work ceases to be creative and becomes simply another skill for children to have at their command. In those expressions in which the creative effort of the individual is given primary emphasis—dramatics, color and form, composition—we may gain understanding of the fundamental personality that is not gained in any other way.

DRAMATICS

The characters that children select to portray satisfy a need for expression. In general, children prefer a dominant role in dramatization. Children live in an adult world in which they are smaller physically, less competent socially, and constantly aware of their immaturity in comparison with adults around them. Consequently a character role that is dominating, at times cruel, and at other times slightly benevolent, serves as a vehicle for emotional release. A still better medium is drama developed by the children out of their own imaginative experiences. The characters chosen depict the predominating moods of the children if they feel "safe" in expressing themselves in the presence of the teacher.

Tense, inhibited children may be fearful of dramatic impersonation. Children who are highly imaginative, but inhibited in their emotional response, may be embarrassed by dramatic expression. To them emotional expression is "not nice," therefore dramatic expression is also taboo. These children may help in formulating the drama but they seldom are chosen by their classmates to be one of the "actors." Teachers may find the use of shadow graphs or puppets helpful in encouraging inhibited children to participate in dramatic expression.

Some children never advance beyond the backdrop of drama. In any dramatic production, casual or more finished, there are characters, such as rabbits, birds, or butterflies, that serve as backdrops for the main characters. We all know how convenient it is to assign the misfits to these impersonations. The children who are always assigned to these generalized characters are aware of the nondescript roles they play. If the teacher has some of these children in her class she should observe carefully to see when they are ready to step out of this role into more active participation.

COLOR AND FORM

Many children lose creative expression in color and form when too great emphasis is placed on realistic reproduction of form. In our elementary schools children are introduced to the media of expression through color and form at the time in their development when they are absorbed in clarifying the external world in which they live. Their dramatic play, for instance, in the primary school consists in playing house, fireman, policeman, and school. In color and form the children depict houses, trees, flowers, and other simple external objects. Day after day many children draw pictures that seem mere duplicates of the ones drawn previously. If at this time art instruction attempts merely to give them techniques for portraying more accurately these external objects, art expression will become a primitive form of draftsmanship and lose all possibility of creative expression. Color rather than form should be emphasized.

When an interest in free experimentation in color is created children begin to relax and enjoy the art period. They find that some colors appeal to them more than others, that their reaction to combinations of color is different from the reaction which they have to any one of the primary colors. This is the beginning of creative expression in art. Form will begin to enter creative expression but more to express a mood than to reproduce an object. Teachers should encourage children to experiment at this level, emphasizing enjoyment of the process with no evaluation of results.

Children are freer with material whose use requires little skill. Children find it easier to portray their ideas when little or no technique is required. Show card or powder paints have largely replaced the little boxes of water colors formerly given to children. Large brushes are substituted for smaller ones. Finger paints are being advocated in place of brush and paint. Thus we have put within the compass of a child's ability more adaptable media of expression.

Repetition of the same mood in color and form may give a clue to a dominant mood in an individual's life. When children have become fully expressive in color and form, one may often see the same mood appearing again and again in their work. The mood may be one of peace, solitude, catastrophe, or joy. These expressions contribute additional evidence which the teacher may utilize in understanding the child's emotional life. On the whole, children gain more satisfaction when they are allowed to portray these moods inconspicuously than when they are asked questions about the meaning of the picture or view the picture on exhibition.

COMPOSITION

Free choice of a topic in composition reveals individual differences. Freedom in selecting a composition topic encourages expression of individual interests and experimentation in style of writing. Though verbal expression in the primary grades may be meager in content and creativity, the foundation is laid at this time for freedom and individuality later.

The content of compositions is often revealing. Content of compositions may reveal a great deal about an individual's fears, wishes, doubts. When a teacher finds a composition that expresses thoughts quite foreign to the child's usual pattern, the composition should be regarded as confidential. An impersonal comment on the paper will reassure the writer that he is safe in developing his thoughts.

2) THE PLAYGROUND

Activity on the playground will be determined by the opportunities offered for physical exercise. If the playground is simply a cleared space with no equipment for playing games, climbing, or jumping, the play will consist of random running and screaming, with subsequent disorganization and fighting. The more active children run, shout, and return from the playground exhilarated and disheveled. Timid children tend to find refuge in a corner, seeking safety from the violence around them. Others dance on the fringe, vicariously enjoying the excitement. The playground period thus becomes an opportunity for display of physical energy, and encourages leadership based on gang tactics. The situation approximates that of the neighborhood gang except that exposure is not limited to those who are interested in the gang.

Undirected play on the playground, though not conducive to constructive activity, presents an opportunity for the teacher to study children's behavior in a primitive and competitive setting. Social acceptance is a primary need of all children; hence awareness of each child's interests and the ability he shows in gaining acceptance by his peers is a basic requirement for planning a sound educational program.

RESPONSE TO PHYSICAL SKILLS

Several factors govern children's ability to compete successfully with their classmates in physical activities. Among these factors are previous opportunity to play freely in games which utilize the large muscles of the body, general motor coordination, body build, and adequate sensory equipment.

By the time children have reached the end of the primary grades they should have had enough experience in large muscle activity to be ready for development of the finer coordinations needed in organized games, such as kick ball, elementary forms of baseball, catching or throwing a soft ball, and such individual activities as skipping rope, skating, and climbing with facility on the jungle gym. The children who enter school without an opportunity to use their bodies freely are at a disadvantage so far as the development of large muscles is concerned. During the first three years of school opportunity must be provided for these children to exercise the large muscles in order to be ready for the more specific skills of the upper elementary school. When opportunity is given for large muscle exercise, adequate motor coordination is normally developed. Children who do not have this opportunity for large muscle development and who begin with small muscle skills are apt to be awkward in attempting the finer skills. They find it difficult to coordinate when attempting to use the eye, hand, and body in a specific skill such as catching a ball.

In addition to muscular development, games which are played on the playground or in the gymnasium require alert sensory responses. The child who is unable to see what is going on cannot make the rapid shifts which are necessary. The child who is unable to hear the general directions which are a part of all physical games is handicapped in cooperating with the team.

Watch for aptitude in skills on the playground in these respects:

1. Facility in adapting to demands of the game: See if there are some children who have difficulty in adapting to change in directions that the game takes. Is this difficulty due to visual or hearing deficiency, faulty motor coordination, or lack of experience in physical activity?
2. Participation in games: See if there are some children who avoid the more complicated games. These children frequently know their own limitations and are still working on large muscle coordination rather than attempting to participate in finer skills. Opportunity should be provided for giving these children the needed experience.
3. Response to specific skills: Try playing kick ball or catching with a volley ball to see the difference in ability among children in your class. The primary school age is an ideal time for developing whatever physical skills the child is ready to learn because in the upper elementary school his acceptance in the group will depend to a certain extent upon his ability to participate in games.
4. Effect of body build: See if you notice any difference in the body build of the children who coordinate their bodies easily and those who appear slower and more awkward in physical sports.

CRITERIA FOR DETERMINING SELF-ASSURANCE

Individual differences may be noted in the degree of assurance children feel in making their way alone with their peers, the code of behavior they have found necessary to develop in order to find a place for themselves, and the extent to which they are accepted by others.

Assurance in any activity is shown by the ease with which a child attacks the experience, his bodily freedom while pursuing it, and his adaptability when unexpected adjustment is required. Children who are in the thick of things, however, are by no means only those who feel assurance. Energetic behavior may indicate that the child is covering his uneasiness by bravado. These children frequently go headlong into an activity. Their one idea is to be noisily and obviously engaged.

Watch for signs of assurance in:

1. The children who maintain leadership after the activity or game has been continuing for five or ten minutes.
2. The children who seem good-natured and relaxed when the activity is finished.
3. The children who have mastered the skill of the game without difficulty.

Watch for signs of lack of assurance in:

1. The children who are noisy but who are on the side lines rather than in the midst of the activity.
2. The children who exert all the energy at their disposal when participating actively in the game.
3. The children who lose interest after the activity has been going on for five or ten minutes.
4. The children who fumble, appear awkward, fall short of what is expected of them in the activity.
5. The children who are touchy, get into frequent arguments, appear irritable.

OUT-OF-SCHOOL ACTIVITIES

Observation of children's behavior in out-of-school activities presents an opportunity to know the kinds of experience children are having and the number of social behaviors they are being required to learn. Neighborhood play, informal or organized clubs, Sunday School, dancing classes, and birthday parties require different kinds of behavior. Children who respond with the same pattern of behavior at birthday parties as in neighborhood play are not adapting to the demands of the situation.

Some children call upon a set pattern in their initial adjustment to every situation. They respond consistently with bravado, rigid dignity, silence, appealing withdrawal, seeming indifference, or calm assurance. Any consistent pattern of social response indicates to the observer the kind of behavior children feel is safest to use. By observing children in various situations the teacher may determine the help they need in social learnings.

SIGNIFICANCE OF SOCIAL PRESSURE

Children's behavior patterns develop through the interaction of their individual emotional and physical constitutions and the pressure exerted on them by the environment in which they are living. Children in our public schools come from many different kinds of environment. They have lived in this environment six years prior to their entrance into school and go back to it when they leave school. Therefore the impact of the neighborhood and the home environment are tremendous factors in developing the patterns of behavior needed for success. If one knows the school district well, location of the child's home will be illuminating in determining the general kind and amount of pressure being placed upon the child.

The neighborhood play is one environmental influence which the school should take into account. It may seem wholesome and absorbing, but close observation may reveal that the neighborhood abounds with destructive influences. Children of primary age may not be fully aware of the activities of the older girls and boys around them, but as they grow out of their egocentric absorption in play they will respond naturally to the stimulation offered by the neighborhood. Only as the school is aware of the destructive influences that will affect children as they grow older, and endeavors to get these children out of the neighborhood into constructive play elsewhere, will it be able to carry on a successful educational program. Children respond gladly to constructive influences if they are allowed freedom of activity in their development.

Home and neighborhood attitudes, expressed interests, daily activities, and forms of amusement have a marked effect on the development of interests. Children unconsciously accept the attitudes and interests observed around them, and by the age of three years begin to imitate the activity and behavior of others. In fact, one may learn a great deal about the family environment by observing the spontaneous dramatic play of young children.

Home and neighborhood may present relatively unified interests, such as predominant encouragement in social living, with frequent visiting between families; steady preoccupation with earning a living and attending to daily chores, with infrequent social contacts; preoccupation with ideas and significance of world events; or many variations of these three diverse centers of interest. Children living in neighborhoods where home and neighborhood express unified interests will follow these interests in their school life unless stimulated to broaden them. These early conditionings must be accepted by the teacher as part of each child's equipment, just as intelligence and personality are accepted.

Children sense that they must be able to cope with their environment if they are going to survive as personalities. They may use predominantly any one of three general patterns of adjustment to environmental demands which are placed upon them.

Wholehearted acceptance of environmental demands. Children may accept wholeheartedly the mores of their environment and attempt to lead other children into the kind of play deemed acceptable. These children are realists. The significant point is that the standards they use become an integral part of their behavior pattern. If the school standards vary decidedly from those of the out-of-school environment, children who conform to the latter will have greater difficulty in adjusting to the school standards than children who participate less wholeheartedly in the community. When there is a wide variation between school and neighborhood standards one is asking an impossible adjustment of these wholehearted neighborhood participants.

Hesitant acceptance of environmental demands. Some children hesitate to accept the codes of behavior set by their out-of-school social groups. At the same time they feel a normal desire to participate in the activities of the group. Children faced with this conflict may remain on the fringe of the activity or decline to participate for a period of time ranging from a year to a few weeks. When normal desire for acceptance in a social group overcomes their hesitancy they may plunge recklessly into group life, following blindly any code of behavior that will gain acceptance for them.

Rejection of environmental demands. Children may reject environmental demands by declining to participate in neighborhood play. This is true of environments in which parents take care that the play is safe and sound according to their standards, as well as in the more rough-and-tumble neighborhoods. Whatever the cause may be, the children who decline to participate in the social life offered to them in out-of-school activities are withdrawing from the demands of the situation in which they find themselves.

Survey the neighborhood attitudes and interests of the children in your class:

1. You may have a heterogeneous group of children, judged on the basis of home and neighborhood environment. By noting their spontaneous expressions of interests and attitudes, you can discover the "indoctrination" from particular neighborhoods.

2. Do the neighborhood patterns and individual personalities of specific children appear in harmony? Children usually adapt very quickly to general home and neighborhood mores, but at times we come across "the square peg" attempting to fit into the circle. These children express interests quite different from those encouraged by their out-of-school environment. We may be assured that any child who expresses interests which diverge markedly from home and neighborhood standards is tending toward becoming a misfit in his environment.

ORGANIZED CLUBS

Communities are beginning to recognize the constructive effect of organized clubs for boys and girls of the upper elementary school age. Various community organizations are responding to this need by providing adequate facilities for wholesome play activities. Schools, churches, and settlement houses are setting aside club rooms with adequate equipment where children may meet under the direction of a lay leader. Such organizations as Boy and Girl Scouts, Y. M. C. A. and Y. W. C. A., men's clubs and women's clubs, are providing directly for improvement of recreational facilities for children and youth or are working for improvement through Community Chest organizations. Facilities for wholesome out-of-school activity have greatly increased, but all too frequently the children who would profit most are not participating in them.

Teachers are in a position to forward the development of children in out-of-school club activity. They may help those children who need more constructive play outlets to find an organization that will interest them. By talking with the club leader or by observing the club in action the teacher may gain further understanding of the interests, emotional maturity, and social adjustment of individual children.

Interests of individual children. The club leader must meet the interests of children if the club is to continue. Therefore he starts with the expressed interests of children and attempts to lead the activity into constructive channels. Activity may range from vigorous sports to long discussions. In some clubs behavior may be decorous, in others so strenuous that to the observer it appears unduly rough. The good leader is fully aware of the response of each child.

Emotional maturity of individual children. The club leader knows which children come regularly and which children show definitely that they have been forced to come because their parents think it is good for them; which children have difficulty in getting to the group because their parents would prefer that they play at home; which children come irregularly, sometimes because they enjoy the feeling of being grown up implied in leaving the neighborhood to join these groups, and at other times because being a little child again is pleasurable.

If the club activities are interesting to the children, one may gauge each child's emotional maturity by the responsibility he takes for attending regularly and his identification with the group when he is there. In girls' clubs one may see the girls who are interested in vigorous sports; the ones who are leaning toward accepted feminine roles of less vigorous activity; the ones who are maturing to the extent that the single sex group is beginning to bore them.

Social adjustment of individual children. The club group is usually much more homogeneous than the school group. Yet children show varying degrees of ability to gain satisfactory recognition from members of the group. Observation and discussion with the group leader will enable the teacher to obtain a clear picture of the patterns of social behavior of individual children.

PARTIES

Teachers usually attend at least one birthday party a year. Being in the position of a guest and in no way responsible for the behavior of the children, the teacher has ample opportunity to observe the situation and the children. Better than at any other time she may become aware of the ideals that parents have for their children.

Party clothes. The clothes that a child wears to parties often reveal to the teacher an aspect of his life previously unknown to her. Boys whom she has always seen in rough clothes may appear in clothes that are strikingly dandified. Girls who have always worn simple, appropriate clothes at school may appear as a "dressed up doll." The teacher can tell by the behavior of these children whether or not "party clothes" are a delight or a nuisance. Some children enjoy the opportunity to play the role indicated by their clothes; others regard them as just so much wearing apparel selected by their parents and therefore make no pretense of changing their behavior to conform to the clothes.

Spontaneity of behavior. Children are generally prepared for behavior appropriate to a party. They usually have been told to be nice to the child who gives the party, to give the present upon arrival, to be sure to take the ice cream or cake nearest and to avoid taking the largest, to thank the hostess before leaving. All these little axioms of good behavior are in opposition to the natural desire of children. It is interesting to see how long they remember the directions given by mother. During the first half hour behavior is so good that it is likely to be stilted; then mother's admonitions are gradually forgotten. The most active period of conflict comes when the refreshments are passed. Only one thought is in the minds of the children present—to get the largest amount, nicely if possible, but to get it. A significant silence reigns as each child struggles with his conscience. Let one child break down and frankly seek the largest portion of ice cream or cake and the securing of refreshments becomes a tussle.

Significance of guest list. Occasionally all children of a class are invited to a particular child's birthday party. In large classes this usually is not feasible, so a selection is made. Since the majority of the children selected are from the same social-economic group, the teacher may see clearly the homogeneous blocks in her class. However, there are usually a few children who do not strictly belong to the homogeneous group. These children are always "nice" children. They are mannerly, usually quiet, are deserving of this honor for one reason or another. Knowledge of the guest lists of every birthday party helps the teacher to become more fully aware of social groupings and possible social tensions in her class group and parent group.

PARENT-TEACHER CONTACTS

Parent-teacher conferences provide a fertile source for gaining insight into the behavior of particular children. In these conferences are two people who are thoroughly familiar with the subject under discussion, namely, the child, and presumably both are interested in the subject. The parent has a cumulative picture of her child gathered over a period of years. The teacher has a cumulative picture gathered over a period of weeks or months. Because the parent's contact covers a longer period her knowledge has great significance. She therefore is the basic informant in the first conference, and a valuable contributor in succeeding conferences.

The information that parents give about their children frequently appears distorted to the teacher. This may be due to one of two reasons. First, the parent, or mother as is usually the case, is uncertain of the teacher's motive in asking for information. She describes the ideal child she wants, thus hoping to give the child a greater chance of securing the teacher's approval. Second, the child's response at home where he is certain of acceptance may be quite different from his response at school where he may feel constrained. The opportunities existing in a particular parent-teacher conference depend upon the ability of the teacher to obtain the confidence and cooperation of the mother.

Teachers often find that they are unable to get the cooperation of some parents. There may be any one of several reasons for this situation. Few teachers in their training were given experience in conducting parent-teacher conferences and in understanding basic techniques that may be used to obtain cooperation. Moreover, certain barriers exist between parent and teachers because of the position each holds in relation to the child and because of their respective positions in the community.

BARRIERS BETWEEN PARENTS AND TEACHERS

Teachers and parents both approach the discussion of a particular child as authorities in their particular realms. Both have vested interests. The teacher wishes to do a good job and to obtain the full help of the parent in doing the work as she sees it. The parent is emotionally identified with her child and wishes to further his development toward the goal that she has in mind. Because the teacher and the parent move in different realms, the goals that they have for the child are often different. Granting this, there is some overlapping of interest which must be found if a plan for the child is to be evolved upon which both parent and teacher can work.

Throughout the school day the teacher is in a position of authority. The children turn to her for help in the solution of their problems. With the parent, on the other hand, the teacher must meet a peer who has ultimate authority over the child and who naturally has strong emotional interests in the child. This precludes telling the parent just how her child should be reared, and demands a give-and-take conference method in which the ideas of both teacher and parent are pooled in order to arrive at a common basis of understanding and cooperation.

A barrier frequently is present between teacher and parent because the social, intellectual, and emotional worlds in which they live may be entirely different. There may be subconscious attitudes toward each other's mode of life which definitely affect ability to establish an understanding and cooperative relationship. Unmarried teachers may subconsciously envy the married woman's role in the social world. The married woman may seem to the teacher to have desirable prestige and emotional satisfactions that she has had to forego. Married teachers may react subconsciously to the seeming advantages that some of the mothers have. They may feel somewhat imposed upon because they cannot take full advantage of their married state in providing a home such as some of these parents are able to maintain. Mothers also may experience envy. They frequently regard teachers as strange human beings but at the same time they may envy the independence and financial freedom which they presume the teacher has. The mother may feel that her life is extremely limited and that she has little prestige and value in the world as compared with the teacher. Only as these two people, the teacher and the parent, see each other as two individuals with similar needs working through their particular jobs as sanely as possible can they come to a mutual understanding.

PARENT AND TEACHER CO-WORKERS IN CHILD EDUCATION

We are fully aware that education in living continues during every hour that the child is awake. School children spend a slightly larger proportion of these hours at home even during the school week. If, in addition, week ends and summer vacations are counted, more education goes on under the direction of parents than under the direction of teachers. To be realistic, education must therefore accept parent responsibility in the process. To ensure education for children that is fundamentally sound teachers and parents must work cooperatively.

The foundation of parent-teacher cooperation lies in the mutual sharing of information, in thinking through together the behavior desired for a particular child, and in working out together methods that may be used at home and at school to obtain the desired results. This procedure places teacher and parent on an equal basis. The teacher, as an educator, assumes the lead in getting the conference off to a good start. It is assumed that the information which each has to give is important.

In your parent conferences have you succeeded in setting up the following situation:

1. One in which parent and teacher are doing about the same amount of "telling."
2. One in which the parent sees that the teacher thoroughly enjoys the interesting behavior of her child.
3. One in which the teacher is able to approve of some attitude or method that the parent is using.
4. One in which the parent becomes more relaxed as the conference continues.

CLUES TO CAUSES OF CHILD'S BEHAVIOR

The general pattern of a child's behavior has been set before he enters school. The teacher can describe the behavior that she sees in school and know that it occurs over and over again, but to understand the cause she must know the roots from which it springs. Parents can give valuable clues to the underlying causes of their children's behavior.

Information about the child's daily schedule. The teacher may learn how much a parent is requiring of a child; whether the schedule is reasonable in relation to the child's age. The part of the day the child enjoys most is a clue to the situation in which relationships are most pleasant.

Information about other members of the family. By learning about other members of the family the teacher can determine where this particular child fits into the family situation. From school records of other children in the family can be learned more accurately just what the child is facing at home.

Information about characteristics of the child that have persisted since infancy. Both strong and weak points may be brought out in this discussion. Often the teacher can find out whether parents consider these characteristics to be hereditary and whether the parents are interested in changing them. Unless some clue to parents' likes and dislikes in behavior is secured, the teacher may try to change a behavior pattern that is admired by the family.

Information about the child's playmates and out-of-school activity. Children may be in a neighborhood where they have ample opportunity to play with children of their own age or the school may offer them the only opportunity for companionship. In the latter case special opportunity for social learnings must be provided by the school.

Information about the classmates, if any, the child sees out of school. This gives an idea which parents are acquainted with one another and to some extent the social group in which the parent moves.

When the teacher has obtained this information or similar information she is ready to select from the child's performance at school and from the interests expressed by the parent the most significant point to discuss with the parent. For example, the teacher may be greatly concerned about the child's social adjustment; the parent, on the other hand, shows no concern in this area but is concerned because the child has a short attention span. If the teacher follows the parent's interest and discusses the short attention span, trying to understand what may cause the difficulty, the question of distraction of interest will inevitably arise. The causes creating distractions will undoubtedly be connected with the child's difficulty in social adjustment. The teacher in this way gains help from the parent in clarifying an area in which she is concerned, but which she has approached through the parent's expressed interest.

Each conference should try to clarify the mutual thinking of teacher and parent on one or two points. Very little is accomplished by trying to cover the child's entire development. The teacher prepares for this conference by thinking through the problem and deciding which aspect of the child's behavior is most significant or most clearly expresses his underlying difficulty. If this sort of thinking goes on before the conference, the teacher will not run the danger of having the conference consumed with the discussion of superficial aspects of behavior.

Analyze your parent conference from the following points:

1. Which conferences have been most helpful? Why?
2. Where have you been able to take your cue from the parent for pursuing discussion of a particular aspect of behavior?
3. What do you find interesting in the child whose parent you are seeing?
4. With which parents do you feel most comfortable? Why?
5. How much have you learned about the parent's attitudes and hopes concerning her child?

SUMMARY

In the foregoing discussion attention has been drawn to opportunities which teachers have for observing the behavior of children in the classroom, on the playground, and in out-of-school activities. Through information gained from parent-teacher contacts valuable supplementary material may be secured that will help the teacher to determine the goals and pressures that are directing the parents' attitudes toward their children. On the basis of the findings from these sources the teacher is able to plan a program for studying more thoroughly the behavior of specific children, and for providing constructive avenues of growth for them.

CHAPTER TWO

How to Study Children's Behavior

OBSERVATION is the principal method to be used in the study of children's behavior. After first-hand observation of their behavior the material may be analyzed in sundry ways. The analysis is of value only to the extent that the observation on which it is based is accurate and unbiased. The teacher has within her grasp the opportunity to make far-reaching contributions to the field of child study. She has daily contact with many individuals living together in a group and grappling with varied situations. If she can learn to observe accurately the human drama before her, no other person is in a position to contribute more to the understanding of children's behavior.

SUGGESTIONS FOR THE STUDY OF BEHAVIOR

USE SCHOOL SITUATIONS TO OBSERVE BEHAVIOR

Several points should be kept in mind when making observations of behavior. All behavior is a response to a situation; it includes not only the response expected but also the effect of any inner pressure that is felt at the time the response is given. We have seen in the preceding chapter that children frequently have inner tensions that interfere, for instance, with giving attention, or that response to a teacher may be colored by the fact that the child is beginning to match his strength against all adults in his environment. Most children give the response that is expected in a situation. Their response is usually appropriate to the requirement. It is this expectation that permits the use of group methods in education. If some children respond inappropriately, we may at once look for divergent pressures placed on these children that are causing confusion. If the teacher keeps in mind, then, that all behavior has a fundamental cause, she may, by keen observation, gain insight into the cause.

1. What situations in your room cause the most divergent responses?
2. How are you gauging whether a response is satisfactory or appropriate?
3. Do you have some children in your classroom who always make the response you expect? Does this seem a good thing for their personality development?
4. Do you have some children who seem consistently to make the wrong response? Can you find the cause?

LEARN TO DESCRIBE BEHAVIOR

Accurate observations can be used again and again, for each observation adds information regarding the child's behavior. It is essential that an observation describe exactly the child's response and the situation in which it occurred. The general tendency is to describe the child's response in terms that are vague or generalized; for instance, "Eleanor worked well all day." "Worked well" may be clearly understood by the teacher who wrote the description, but when the record becomes old it may be impossible to say just what "worked well" meant. It might mean working well in comparison with the work Eleanor did on other days, or in comparison with other members of the class. Also, what one teacher may consider working well, another teacher might deem unacceptable.

An accurate record requires that the situation and the response be described specifically. For example, "Donald started off this morning in one of his serious moods. When he entered the classroom in the morning he did not look at anyone. He went to his desk. When he was settled he looked at me. His eyes were dull, his face was white. He did not smile but waited passively for the work to begin." This description gives an exact portrayal of Donald's behavior on a particular morning.

Should this behavior occur often the teacher would be justified in assuming that Donald is distressed over some aspect of his life.

Try writing down observations:

1. Avoid the use of words that indicate good or bad behavior, such as cooperative, lazy, bothersome, charming. These words describe a judgment already made.
2. Describe exactly what the child did that caused you to conclude that he was cooperative, etc., rather than merely stating the observation as a fact.
3. Describe behavior that occurs frequently and see what different situations cause that particular response.
4. Observe one particular situation and see how many different responses you are able to distinguish among the various children in the class.

STUDY CUMULATIVE DESCRIPTIONS OF BEHAVIOR

Single observations are always interesting but are of doubtful value for drawing conclusions with regard to possible causes of behavior. If the one observation is found to be characteristic of the child's behavior, it may, of course, be considered more seriously. Cumulative records of behavior are more accurate, however, because they provide a better sample of behavior on the good days as well as on poor days, in teacher directed activity and spontaneous activity, in gay moods and serious moods.

Cumulative descriptions of behavior and the situations in which the behavior occurs make it possible to study cause-and-effect relationships. If the cause and the effect are obvious in the outer situation and the child has made the completely appropriate response, these may be accepted on their face value. The observations that should receive closest scrutiny are those where the response is at variance with the cause or stimulation. In these the teacher may see the pressures exerted by feelings and interests of the child's personal and emotional life. She is therefore better able to understand the kind of opportunities that the particular child needs.

1. Begin to collect descriptions of behavior of children in a variety of situations. Study these cumulative records from time to time in order to clarify personality needs.
2. Some few minutes spared each day from *directing* children's behavior to *studying* behavior will bring encouraging results in wiser and more efficient classroom management. Often this will aid in determining solutions to troublesome problems.
3. Be particularly aware of repeated patterns of behavior. These stereotypes indicate that the child is falling back on a response he considers safe whether or not it is one that is particularly adapted to the situation.

CHILD'S DEVELOPMENTAL AGE

Developmental age is the level of development a child has reached regardless of his chronological age. A child of eight years may be developmentally eight in all areas of growth, but this is rather exceptional. Large numbers of children measure lower or higher in their intellectual development than their real age. Fifty per cent of the child population show intellectual development relatively near their chronological age; the remaining fifty per cent show a widening difference between their age and their intellectual development. Physical, social, and emotional development show the same difference in relation to chronological age, but there are few accurate measures for determining these developments. We are, however, able to measure academic achievement, which we know shows wide variation from age expectancy. A nine-year-old girl recently tested for intellectual development and achievement showed in these areas the development of a fourteen-year-old. In emotional development she was somewhat in advance of her real age, but in physical and social development she was a little girl of ten. The majority of children in a classroom will show some discrepancy in the several areas of development, and a few may show as marked discrepancy as this child. It is possible to gauge approximately the various levels of physical, intellectual, social, and emotional development of children by using simple clues.

CLUES FOR DISCOVERING PHYSICAL DEVELOPMENTAL AGE

HEIGHT IN RELATION TO WEIGHT AND AGE

A child's height alone provides no indication of developmental age, but when it is considered in relation to weight and age it is found that children range from low limits of expectancy to high limits. The height-weight-age expectancy of a particular child may be determined by referring to height-weight-age tables accessible through the school's health department. By six years of age children usually have set the relative pace in physical growth that they will keep through early adolescence. Tall children continue to be taller than the average and on the whole tend to mature physically earlier than the shorter, more slowly growing children. The children who are growing rather uniformly in the other areas of growth present no particular difficulty, but these fast growing children who are not growing socially, intellectually, or emotionally at the same rate as physically face the difficulty of being unequally developed individuals when they reach physical maturity.

1. Observe closely the children who seem to be large for their age. Are they forging ahead equally in achievement, social maturity, and emotional control? Approximately how much difference is there between their level of development in the various areas of growth?
2. Which children in your class show most uniform development? Do these children seem more reliable than those developing less evenly?
3. Do some children seem to be developing more slowly physically than in other areas of growth? Does this discrepancy in growth produce emotional or social disturbances?

MOTOR COORDINATION

The motor coordination of children during the elementary school years is more efficient than during the rapid growing periods of preschool and adolescent growth. Though many coordinations are still underdeveloped, the fact that growth is proceeding at a relatively even rate is conducive to smooth coordination at the level of the child's physical maturity.

As stated previously, during the preschool years control of

the larger muscles of the body develops rapidly if children are given an opportunity to exercise these muscles. However, many children enter the kindergarten who have had very restricted activity and therefore their large muscles have not received exercise.

Development of motor coordination may be observed in the primary grades by checking on the ease with which children go down stairs. Do they step down with the same foot rather than with alternate feet? Do they hold to the banister or to someone when they use alternate feet? Children know their physical capabilities. They adapt their response to the controls in which they have confidence.

Manual coordination may be noted in the ease with which children use a large paintbrush and paints, the way they use a hammer, the efficiency with which they use a saw. In the primary grades a child should use a large paintbrush in a relaxed way. He should not need to use his tongue, his face muscles, and even his toes to paint the lines he wishes.

Finer coordinations are needed in reading and writing. Reading, particularly, requires a number of coordinated activities: eyes must focus together or fuse in looking at the printed word, the book must be held at the distance most conducive to clear vision, attention must be paid to the meaning of the words. In oral reading attention must be paid to the reading of others, comments of teacher, and pronunciation of words. This is a complicated task for six-year-olds, who often are not developed well enough to manage these coordinations. They avoid reading or appear disinterested because the physical strain produces discomfort.

Group the children in your class roughly on the basis of development in the following motor coordinations:

1. Ease with which they manage large muscle activities, such as running, jumping, and skipping.
2. Their degree of relaxation in finer coordinations required in reading, writing, and spelling. Effort should be noticeable only in the part of the body required for the activity. If the entire body is tense, the child may be attempting a skill that is too difficult for his level of physical development.

3. Evidence of fatigue after work requiring finer muscle coordination. This may be shown by increase in restlessness, twitching of parts of the body, increased irritability.
4. Level of skill individual children are able to attain in large or fine muscular coordination with relatively little strain.

PHYSICAL SKILL IN DRESSING AND CARE OF BELONGINGS

Every teacher in the primary grades is familiar with the inept children whose clothing is continually parting company, whose coats are always on the floor, whose shoe laces are constantly coming untied, and who in general become disorganized easily.

Children at six years of age are usually sufficiently developed physically to put on their own coats, but many children in the third grade still struggle with this task. Normally a child of six can tie his own shoe laces though he is still in the learning stage. And yet, if the teacher is in a hurry one may observe her tying the shoe laces of children in the fourth grade.

Buttons should be managed easily, if they are large, by children in the first or second grades. The ease with which buttons are buttoned is a significant clue to motor development.

1. Which children in your class have attained complete independence in care of belongings and dressing?
2. In what areas of care for belongings are some of your children still having difficulty?
3. Which children appear disorganized in caring for personal possessions? What do you consider the reasons for this disorganization?

CLUES FOR DETERMINING INTELLECTUAL DEVELOPMENT

ABILITY TO FOLLOW DIRECTIONS

Ability to follow directions requires intellectual capacity to comprehend the directions, to remember enough detail to carry them through, and to associate the directions with the particular task at hand. By the age of six children should be able to follow three directions when the situation is made concrete and the directions are carried out immediately. Frequently the number and scope of directions given by a teacher are beyond the intellectual capacity of many children.

1. Are there some children in your class who have difficulty in following directions? Is this due to inability to comprehend or to difficulties in remembering the directions?
2. With which children does ability to follow directions relate to intellectual ability or achievement level?
3. Do some children derive pleasure from following directions meticulously? Is this desirable?

RELATION OF ACADEMIC ACHIEVEMENT TO INTELLECTUAL DEVELOPMENT

Children's achievement in relation to grade norms is of course an important measuring rod in determining intellectual development. If this criterion alone is used, however, the evaluation may prove inaccurate.

Because of poor physical development children may be unable to coordinate hand, eye, and attention in an activity such as reading. Some children, well coordinated and compliant, may be able to achieve a great deal in relation to their intellectual ability because their physical, emotional, and intellectual organism is operating uniformly toward the goal. On the other hand, children who find it difficult to make the necessary coordinations required for a task, or children who are antagonistic to adults, although intellectually as capable as the first group, are hindered in their achievement because the organism is not unified in working toward the goal.

1. Do you have some children who appear bright but who remain retarded in academic achievement? Are there discrepancies of growth in emotional, social, or physical development?
2. Which children in your class are achieving up to their intellectual capacity?

DEVELOPMENT OF INTERESTS

Children differ in their interests and in the intensity with which they pursue them. Generally, children of high intelligence are able to pursue a greater number of interests with intensity than children of average or below average intelligence. The teacher, however, may notice that some very intelligent children have many interests which they follow spasmodically and superficially. This behavior indicates a scattering of attention due to some personal discomfort, usually in the emotional life of the child.

Throughout the elementary school years children should be encouraged to develop many interests because through these they explore the world around them. All interests, however, will not be pursued with equal intensity. Many children show a predominant interest early in their school life and continue to grow in skill and ingenuity as they work on it year after year. An example of this is a child who in the first grade is interested in airplanes. By the sixth grade his crude attempts at constructing an airplane have developed to the extent that he can construct meticulous and exact reproductions of various types of miniature planes.

In your class, note:
1. Which children have the most complex interests? Do these interests appear in line with their general intellectual ability and achievement?
2. Which children have meager interests? Is this due to lack of stimulation, scattered attention, or low intellectual development?
3. How much initiative is shown by individual children in pursuing their interests? If there are differences in initiative, can you account for them?

ABILITY IN ABSTRACT THINKING

As children develop intellectually, they should be able to deal with abstract ideas more accurately. Until the last decade we grossly exaggerated children's ability to think in abstract terms. We now know that children of primary age need to return to concrete experiences again and again in order to achieve real understanding. They may know how to count to 50, but their comprehension may not extend beyond the quantity 5. By the upper elementary grades, however, they should be able to project their ideas beyond the concrete. They begin to visualize conditions of living, for example, that are quite different from their own. Children in the upper elementary grades who must still rely on concrete experiences rather than language for clear comprehension of an idea are operating on the primary level in this area of intellectual ability.

1. Which children in your class have reached the stage where they can comprehend an idea clearly through language alone? Have you checked on the accuracy of the concept they have formed?
2. Which children show greater interest when ideas are presented concretely through materials?
3. Which children explore abstract ideas spontaneously? In what kind of abstract ideas are they interested? Is this because they have matured intellectually to this level or because they have stimulation from adult companionship?

ABILITY TO RESERVE JUDGMENT

Children in the primary grades tend to reach conclusions on the basis of limited examination of the facts. They will decide, for instance, that Jimmy should not be allowed to care for the turtles because he neglected them once. In the upper elementary grades children would take a great deal more into account before coming to such a conclusion. They would be able to weigh the circumstances that led to Jimmy's forgetting to attend to the turtles.

Again, children in the primary grades will respond with enthusiasm to plans that are presented as interesting. Children on the upper elementary level will wish to know more specifically what the plan holds for them, and then will wish to decide on the basis of alternative suggestions whether or not they will accept the original plan.

1. Have you noticed among children in your class individual differences in reserving judgment? How do you account for these differences?
2. Do some children appear annoyed when being helped to see various angles of a situation before pronouncing judgment?
3. Are some children unable to make a judgment even when an adequate amount of information has been obtained? Can you account for their indecision?

AWARENESS OF DETAIL

As children grow in intellectual ability they tend to see more detail in the world around them or in an object they are studying. This is shown clearly in the detail with which ships are drawn after a visit to one. When working with wood a kindergarten child is satisfied with making a flat board with bow and stern, a few smokestacks, and perhaps a solid piece of wood for the cabin. A child in the fourth grade often will work meticulously to put in portholes, cabin windows, masts, pilot house, and numerous other details. Development in ability to note detail indicates that children are comprehending more completely the significance of detail in the total concept.

1. Try having your class draw a picture of a man. Notice the differences in the amount of detail in the various drawings.[1]
2. Do some children lose sight of their goal because they become immersed in detail? How do you account for this?
3. Do some children fail to see the significance of particular pieces of work because they have failed to note details?

EXPRESSION OF IDEAS

Ability to express ideas is closely related to ease in language expression. However, there are many children and adults who talk a great deal but express relatively few ideas. Expression of ideas is the ability to make another person understand the thought in the speaker's mind. Experience in expressing one's ideas directly affects the ability to do so. If opportunity is given in the classroom, intellectual development may be judged on the basis of learning that takes place in the development of this skill rather than in achievement at the time of entrance to the class.

1. Which children in your class are most fluent in expressing their ideas? Is this fluency due to superior intellectual ability, stimulation at home, large vocabulary, or self-confidence?
2. Are some children more fluent in writing or dictating ideas than in general discussion? Why?
3. Does the level of comprehension of some children seem far in advance of their ability to convey their ideas to others? What is causing this discrepancy?

MEMORY

As children grow older the method they use to remember facts or principles changes. During the primary age they try to remember almost completely by rote. They carry the gen-

[1] Goodenough, Florence. *Measurement of Intelligence by Drawings.* World Book Company, Yonkers-on-Hudson, N. Y., 1926.

eral image and recall it as accurately as possible. As they gain more and more experience, however, they find this type of memory is inaccurate. They begin to organize their facts around particular cues. This is especially noticeable in the development of spelling ability. The primary child sees words as wholes and learns them more or less accurately. As he approaches the upper elementary grades and his spelling vocabulary increases, he must learn to break down these words into phonetic units, otherwise his accuracy in spelling is unpredictable. It is important, therefore, to observe the system children are building for accurate memory as closely as we observe the results of memory. A sound memory system is not being developed if after the age of eight or nine a child depends entirely on his ability to recall a memory whole.

A second aspect of memory is the period that may elapse between the initial experience and accurate recall of the experience, that is, the memory span. It is assumed that the period between the initial learning and the recall of this learning will increase with growth in intellectual ability. Young children in the primary grades usually are able to remember from one day to another the major points of any activity in which they are interested. They seldom can drop the idea completely and recall it accurately after several days. The upper elementary school child has progressed to the point where he may recall accurately after several weeks have elapsed. He has begun to build up a logical organization for memory of fact. We may, however, expect at all ages great individual differences.

Several factors contribute to accuracy of recall and length of memory span. First, initial learning must be accurate if the memory is to be retained over a period of time. Lack of attention will cause inaccuracy of learning, and as a result the recall will be inaccurate. Second, there must be "desire" to remember an experience or such strong emphasis that the experience cannot be forgotten. If children have had many painful experiences they may unconsciously avoid retention of the memory of them. They give fleeting attention to many initial experiences and go on to the next experience as quickly as possible. Because these children secure a vague initial impression, their recall or memory is inaccurate. At the other extreme are children who find great security in organizing facts as they learn them. They derive intense satisfaction from being able to recall these facts accurately, and therefore build through experience rather a prodigious memory.

1. Are there some children in your class who give scant attention to initial learnings and therefore learn inaccurately?
2. Have you tried having children analyze the methods they use in trying to remember experiences accurately?
3. Have you tried giving children definite cues for aid in recall?

CLUES FOR DETERMINING SOCIAL DEVELOPMENT

METHODS USED IN SOCIAL CONTACT

Children of preschool age initiate social contacts through physical contact with other children. They begin by handing materials to one another, by pushing, pulling, slapping, biting. They are able to conduct a monologue, but give and take in conversation is not possible. One may see this same pattern when a young child begins to talk over the telephone. He is able to talk to the person at the other end of the wire, but rarely hears what the other person says to him.

Gradually through the preschool years children begin to use language for the exchange of ideas. However, even through the primary grades, some children are unable to listen to other children when they are speaking, or resort to physical contact if no one pays heed to their verbal request. By the upper elementary grades social contact through language should be possible. Children should be able to listen to their classmates and to manage exchange of ideas through speech. Nevertheless, even in the upper elementary school there are some children who can express their ideas, but who are still unable to participate in a real discussion.

1. Which children in your class are able to make their social contacts primarily through language?
2. Are some children good talkers but poor listeners? What is their general level of development?

3. Must some children have physical contact through punching, grabbing, and similar methods in order to make a satisfactory social contact?

SIGNIFICANCE OF SEX GROUPINGS

Boys and girls play together naturally through the preschool years and early primary grades unless the school superimposes boy-girl segregation for various activities. Approximately at the age of seven or eight segregation according to sex occurs spontaneously. Boys are definitely showing interest in more vigorous activities. They are becoming aware of their masculine differences. Girls also are becoming interested in and identified with their own sex. By the upper elementary school age the social codes which children are developing usually exclude members of the opposite sex in group play. Just before puberty boy groups and girl groups appear to be strongly antagonistic. Teasing of groups of the opposite sex occurs, and great disdain is expressed for the other sex group.

1. Which children are adhering to the development expected in sex groupings? Does this development follow physical and intellectual development rather closely?
2. In the upper elementary school do you have some children who still wish to play predominantly with the opposite sex? How are these children accepted?

CONTRIBUTION TO GROUP ACTIVITY

Children vary normally in the interest they have in group activity. Normal social development, however, assumes that interest in other persons will progress from social contacts made on an egocentric basis to contacts made because of shared interest. Throughout the preschool period and early primary years interest in group activity is primarily directed toward self-satisfaction. Children will participate in group play as long as they are receiving recognition that is pleasing to them. As soon as displeasure is felt they leave the group. Beginning at approximately the age of nine they show a distinct desire to be included in some group, large or small. Exclusion from all groups creates in them a feeling of inadequacy and isolation. Acceptance of the obligation of contributing to a group is the most important learning that occurs during the primary grades. Children are accepted in the home usually on the basis of their own personalities. In a group they are accepted only on the nature of their contribution. By the upper elementary school age children are isolated from the group if they have not learned to make a contribution. At this time special skills, particularly in the physical activities, prove distinct assets. The case of Jerome on page 51 illustrates one method that children will use when they have not learned to make a group contribution.

It is not the amount of time spent in group activity that is significant in understanding children's social behavior but the quality of participation the individual child shows when playing with a group. Social learnings occur and satisfactions accrue when children are vital, contributing members of a group. Any child who is simply endured in a group or who participates vicariously while standing on the fringe of activity is gaining no fundamental satisfaction. Instead of developing interest in group activity these non-participants are building up a sense of failure. Self-consciousness and timidity in social relations develop when no recognition is secured after an effort has been made to enter group play. Normally, by the age of nine or ten children should have found out through experience and guidance the contribution they can make.

1. Are there children in your class who remain in group activity only so long as they can "have their own way"?
2. Are some children always active participants in group play? How do they manage their social relations?
3. Which children seem to be always on the fringe of activity? Do they ever have the satisfaction of being included even briefly in the play? What contribution do they make at these times?
4. Are there children in your class who are isolated from child-directed activity? How do they behave under such circumstances?

CODES THAT GOVERN CHILDREN'S SOCIAL BEHAVIOR

Children come to school at the age of six with rudimentary codes of social behavior developed from their experiences at home and in neighborhood play. These codes range from adult standards of social behavior that encourage children to talk over difficulties, to give other children a fair chance, to be considerate of others, and to share playthings, to primitive codes developed by the children themselves, such as "might makes right," "take what you can," "bully the small fellow," and similar aggressive methods. In unsupervised play the primitive codes developed by children are likely to predominate. Children who have adopted adult codes as their own are at a distinct disadvantage unless they have leadership ability to convince other children of the value of using them.

Adult codes. Children who are in the game but who continually shout that "the play is not fair, you can't do that" are attempting to act on an adult level. These children usually resent rough-and-tumble play.

Children who avoid rough-and-tumble games are also attempting to act on an adult level. Dignity governs their behavior. They exchange ideas through conversation or participate in mild exercise.

Children who insist on playing the game the "correct" way are adopting an adult code. They become disgusted with childish interpretations of such games as baseball, hockey, and football. "Either the real game or none at all for them."

Age level codes. Children in the primary grades are more interested in achieving the goal than in playing according to rule. When faced with a possible loss of goal, they tend to use "unfair" methods. Starting a little ahead of time in the game; inconveniencing one's opponent, stepping into a more advantageous position when unnoticed are the usual transgressions.

In the upper elementary school, a sense of fair play and justice is being developed. A child whose behavior is distinctly unfair is not accepted by other children—but behavior unacceptable to adults may not be unacceptable to children. Fair and just play still allows for "bullying the underdog."

LEADERSHIP AMONG CHILDREN

Leadership in the primary grades is held by those children who through their ingenuity and ability to bring other children into their plans are able to keep an activity going. As soon as boys and girls begin to play predominantly with their own sex, other qualities of leadership are demanded. Boys give leadership on the basis of physical prowess, skill in sports, initiative in organizing games, and fair play in the game. Girls generally place less emphasis on physical prowess for their leaders but they consider ability in games an asset. Ingenuity and ability to share their plans and "secrets" are more conspicuous elements in the choice of a leader than fair play, ability in games, or physical strength. During the upper elementary school years children are evolving their codes of behavior and therefore they choose a leader who expresses through behavior the qualities they accept.

CLUES FOR DETERMINING EMOTIONAL DEVELOPMENT

DEPENDENCE ON PERSONAL APPROVAL

Dependence on the opinion of others, either adults or peers, is characteristic of young children. After the first weaning from home when children enter the kindergarten or first grade, dependence on adults should decrease rapidly. However, there are many children who feel little security in their own abilities and require a great deal of reassurance from adults in order to gain independence from them. It is not possible to demand independence in these children. The only solution is to create in them confidence in their own ability. One would think that capable children would develop independence normally, but capable children sometimes are also very critical and highly sensitive. Under these circumstances, confidence develops more slowly and reassurance from the adult is a necessity.

The majority of children in the upper elementary school will accept the necessity of independence from the adult. They have found through experience that the adult is annoyed by their demands for reassurance. If they should still need reassurance they will attach themselves to the more independent members of the class. They frequently are the "handy men" of the class, willing to do any chore in order to be rewarded by approval. These children will laboriously print the charts after other children have had the fun of planning them. They go after the necessary playground equipment while other children are enjoying the game. They will be the "housekeepers of the class."

The Case of Fred

Fred is an excellent example of a capable boy who still desired to be dependent on the teacher, but who had accepted the fact that his dependence would not be tolerated. He still tried in many ways to gain the teacher's approbation. He was the most polite boy in the class. Whenever visitors entered, he was the first to offer chairs to them. He was constantly on the lookout for opportunities to be considerate to other members of the class. His pencils were offered, his best eraser would be given freely to any child who needed one. He would step out of first place in line, which he always was able to secure because he was alert to the situation, in order to give it to another child. Although able to make excellent contributions in discussion, he would gladly keep quiet if a child whom he admired wished to contribute first. His entire activity showed the need for recognition from the teacher and children.

GROWTH IN ABILITY TO EXPRESS GRADATIONS
IN EMOTIONAL RESPONSE

The emotional response of preschool children is characterized by an "all-or-none" reaction. Their joy is extravagant and uncontrolled; their anger is violently expressed. In the primary grades children have begun to experience happiness and contentment as well as joy. They give expression to irritability and annoyance more frequently than to violent anger. They may become sober or silent rather than dejected in their sadness. Changes from one mood to another are less sudden, and the dominant mood is sustained for a longer period of time. Children who come to school happy and contented are able to maintain the mood for a relatively long time even when faced with adverse conditions.

Children in the elementary school seldom express violent anger, though forceful indignation may be shown. The child who loses control in anger and resorts to the more primitive tantrum is usually regarded with distrust by the other children. Unfortunately, exuberance is regarded also with some distrust as our cultural mores frown upon expression of intense emotion. This produces a leveling of emotional expression. Many persons believe that a process of socialization of emotions in which only bland expression of feeling is tolerated is unfortunate. Control of emotions is required in a social world, but it should not be gained at the expense of warm emotional response.

1. Are there children in your class who have difficulty in controlling their emotional responses?
2. Do some children resort to tantrums at home but exercise control in school?
3. Are some children regarded askance by their classmates because they express emotion vigorously? Have you found a legitimate avenue of expression for these responses?
4. Are there some children whose moods fluctuate during the day?

RESPONSE TO PROBLEM SITUATIONS

A problem situation implies that an individual working in a situation meets an obstacle that hinders his advance toward the goal he has in mind. The degree of emotional response created under these circumstances is in direct relationship to the interest he has in obtaining his goal. Growth toward emotional maturity assumes that the individual works toward a solution of the problem. While recognizing his emotional response he withholds action until he has thought through the situation. Growth toward this degree of emotional maturity proceeds slowly. Individual variation is marked.

Children in the elementary school show decided individual differences when confronted with problem situations intense enough to create an emotional response. Patterns of response used in problem situations develop during the preschool years. In general, four distinct patterns may be observed:

1. The attempt to solve the problem alone by such methods as trial and error or thoughtful consideration of the problem.
2. The attempt to solve the problem by securing help from more experienced persons.
3. The evasion of the problem by ignoring the situation and turning to something more interesting, or by haphazard or partial solution.
4. The denial of the problem by assuming a "sour grapes" attitude.

Children who early develop a pattern of attacking a problem through thoughtful consideration of it are well started on their way toward emotional maturity. Children who evade a problem or deny it should receive help from the teacher in developing confidence and skill in attacking the problems which confront them.

1. Analyze the responses that individual children make to problem situations. Which of the four approaches do they use predominantly?
2. To what extent does emotional disturbance and fatigue affect the response children use in attacking a problem?
3. Have you situations in your room that stimulate ingenuity and logical approach to problem situations?

ACCEPTANCE OF FRIENDLY ADVANCES

We have seen that the usual trend of relationships with others is toward the establishment of friendly give and take of ideas and services. Because children derive a sense of prestige when making contributions to a group or to a person, they often contribute to others more easily than they are able to accept friendliness. Acceptance of friendliness requires an emotional response to the person who makes the advance. In their ability to accept friendliness children show individual differences which usually portray a fundamental difference in personality pattern. There is apparent little developmental sequence but rather a personality pattern that is established early and grows in complexity as children mature.

1. Have you observed some children who are over-eager in their acceptance of friendly advances and therefore embarrass the person making the advance?
2. Have you noticed some children who respond with a blank expression or embarrassment to friendly advances made by others?
3. Are there some children in your class who receive friendly overtures from children and adults? What in their personality invites these overtures?

RESPONSE TO TIME REQUIREMENTS

In the primary grades children generally have little awareness of time requirements. An ordered day, however, gives them fundamental satisfaction and a sense of security, if the time allotments are not set too rigidly. Even at this early age, however, individual differences become apparent. There are some children who are able to shift quickly from one activity to another and so are prepared for the new activity. There are others who have difficulty in closing one interest and becoming prepared for the next. Children in the upper elementary grades usually have developed an awareness of time requirements, although here too the ability to shift from one interest to another quickly shows great individual variation. Some children "warm up" to an activity slowly; others mobilize their energies rapidly.

In addition to individual differences in emotional motility there are two general factors that influence a child's ability to conform to time requirements: first, the presence of fatigue, and second the degree of egocentricity. Presence of fatigue has a direct effect on readiness to accept time requirements. A child who is fatigued usually pursues his activity at a rate he can manage. Since greater energy is required to make a shift in activity and follow the tempo set by others, he tends to make the shift slowly. Egocentric children may become so absorbed in their own interests that they pay little heed to time requirements set by others. They are not conscious of group requirements and therefore attend to their own interests whether or not the group requirements mean a shift.

1. Are there some children in your class who are always ready for a shift in activity? Why?
2. Are there some who are aware of group requirements to the point of limiting their own activity as necessary?
3. Which children have difficulty in closing their activities and are always the late ones?
4. With any of these responses what relationship do you see to temperamental differences or general health?

SIGNIFICANCE OF EGOCENTRIC BEHAVIOR

The period of infancy represents the highest point of egocentric behavior. Until the age of two and a half or three children view everything in their environment on the basis of their interests and desires. Egocentricity diminishes very slowly until about the age of eight, when group consciousness begins to develop. We have noted above the struggle which children go through when they try to decide whether their own desires are worth sacrificing in order to be included in the group. A normal child will always consider the satisfaction he is able to achieve by being a member of a group. Denial of self or non-egocentricity is abnormal.

1. Are there some children in your class who are acutely aware of themselves under all situations, that is, evidence self-consciousness though not necessarily embarrassment?
2. Which children have developed a sound balance between compliance to group wishes and expression of own personality?
3. Will some of the children, in their desire for group acceptance, deny their own needs for satisfaction?

PERSONAL-SOCIAL RELATIONS IN THE CLASSROOM

SIGNIFICANCE OF PERSONAL-SOCIAL RELATIONS

Personal-social relations permeate all activity throughout the life span of human beings. (Disturbances in personal-social relations affect the output of individuals from the age of four to the end of life.) For this reason sound development in personal-social relations should be the chief goal of our educative process. Normal adjustment in personal-social relations should enable the individual to fit into most groups, to sense the contributions he can make, and to gain from these groups a satisfactory response. This implies a thinking, feeling individual who both gives and receives emotional satisfaction in relations with others.

Basically, relation with other individuals reflects the attitude the person has about himself. If he is unsure of himself but has found it necessary to deny this problem situation, he will assume an air of bravado that usually rebuffs other people. Needing reassurance in his personal relations he forestalls consideration from others by the very tactics he uses—bragging, making dogmatic statements of opinions, always having an answer he assumes to be correct. The individual who is relatively self-confident, who is aware that he has a contribution to make in his social relations, usually is able to express naturally his consideration of other people. He is freer to give and receive because he is emotionally comfortable. The person who is conscious of his inabilities or who obviously lacks self-confidence carries his difficulty on his sleeve. Often these people will be apologetic. They have a cringing approach to others. Instead of being pitied and reassured, they are avoided and ignored.

In these three general types of attitudes about the self, we see the development of patterns in personal-social relations that have a profound effect on the satisfactions an individual derives from contacts with others.

1. Can you identify those children in your class who are emotionally secure in their personal-social relations?
2. Are there some children who are rebuffed in their social relations because of the bravado they assume in their social contacts?
3. Are there some children who are ignored by their classmates because they are apologetic and cringing in their social relations?

CHILDREN'S RELATIONSHIPS WITH ONE ANOTHER

By the time they reach the upper elementary school children usually have a well-defined pattern of behavior in their group relationship. If the pattern is one that encourages a satisfying response from their classmates, we may assume that these children are making a normal social adjustment. In our American culture we are prone to consider normal social adjustment as exemplified in vigorous group activity. We assume that every person has a normal desire to be a member of a large group and, if at all possible, to be a leader in the group. As we watch the development of children's social relationships, many normal types of social adjustment are evident. We may observe the roles of leader, intelligent follower, blind follower, nonparticipant in large groups, spontaneous participant in small groups, quiet contributor, and "handy man." All these adjustments are normal, with the exception, perhaps, of the blind follower and the handy man. The blind follower is losing awareness of his own interests and needs. The pressure for group acceptance has overshadowed his individuality. Children who do the "dirty work" for the group and who are always the ones called upon in an emergency derive some satisfaction from this position, but the position is scarcely one to create a feeling of self-esteem.

Children should have experience in both large and small groups. Some children who are followers in a large group may develop leadership in small groups and particularly in activities of their own choice. By following leaders of large groups intelligently, they learn a great deal about group cooperation and the workable tactics of leadership. Some children are by temperament retiring and gentle. The "hullabaloo" of the large group is distracting. These children may seek solitary work more frequently than others, but if they are able to cooperate in small groups their adjustment is normal and signifies only a temperamental difference. These children need protection from continuous contacts with large groups and planned opportunity to experience satisfactions that they derive from working with small groups.

1. Have you noticed children in your class who find participation in large groups distracting?
2. Are there some children in your class who seem to derive happiness from a limited number of contacts with other children?
3. Which children seem to conform to the generally accepted pattern in social adjustment of continuous and vigorous participation in group activity?

PRESTIGE AS A FACTOR IN PERSONAL-SOCIAL RELATIONS

Social prestige has little significance to children in the primary grades, but during the upper elementary grades it begins to have an effect on personal-social relations. Children begin to notice the children who come to school in a "large" car, who have more spending money than the others, who possess more intriguing pencils or any other belonging that is desired at this age. The children possessing these "advantages" may use them as sources of power. They secure power principally by bestowing favors. The favor may be including special friends in a select group, inviting a favored few to the corner drugstore with the pennies jingling enticingly, or parting with some unique possession to a favorite.

Upper elementary school children with greater social prestige than other members of the class may begin to utilize this superiority. They have enough social awareness to be cautious in the use they make of their social prestige. The children who secure power through social prestige are usually those who have not gained acceptance of the group through legitimate contribution. Careful observation of children who gather small groups around them without having previously shown leadership in ideas or ability usually reveals social prestige as the basis of the leadership.

The Case of Jerome

Jerome came into the fourth grade at a distinct disadvantage. His education the three previous years had been in Italy. He could speak English but would often hesitate for the exact word he wished to use. He was unacquainted with the slang terms used by the children. His academic work was below the work of the other children. Though a vigorous boy, his unfamiliarity with American games made him somewhat an outsider on the playground. Try as he would he was unable to gain a place in the group satisfactory to him. About the first of the year after he had been in school for several months he seemed to be making headway with a few children. However, his ability to contribute showed little change. A chance meeting in the corner drugstore solved the mystery. Jerome entered the store, hands in pockets, followed by four eager classmates. Ten minutes were taken to dispense the favors that could be bought for five cents.

FRIENDSHIPS

For many years we have looked askance upon close friendships among children. However, we know at the present time that in the upper elementary school and junior high school close friendships indicate a normal developmental sequence from egocentric interests to interest in others. Friendships from approximately nine to fourteen years are usually with members of the same sex and are absorbing for a period of time—sometimes as long as several years. As long as contacts are maintained with other children and the two friends do not become exclusively absorbed in each other the development is wholesome. It is true that friends may wish always to work together, to be seated together in the classroom, to be on the same team in all games. At times, one friend seems to dominate the other. This may be a shift on the part of the dependent child from dependence on adults to dependence on someone of his own age. If this is true, we can expect that it is only a developmental step that will lead into wider relationships. The child who has no particular friend should receive our concern in the upper elementary grades rather than the child who has a particular "buddy."

1. Which children in your class show a tendency for absorbing friendships? What appears to be the basis of interest in their friendships?
2. Do these close friends work cooperatively with others?
3. Does this close friendship dominate destructively the relationship of other children with them?
4. Which children seem to develop no strong friendships and appear to be unchosen when team selections are made?

SIGNIFICANCE OF AGGRESSIVE BEHAVIOR

Children who are aggressive and nonconformists in their behavior usually consume an undue proportion of the teacher's time because they disrupt classroom routine. These children desire the limelight, they demand attention from the teacher, and are able to work for only a limited period of time without supervision.

UNDERLYING CAUSES

Patterns of behavior encouraged at home may be one cause of aggression. Encouragement of this type of social response may be due to confusion on the part of the parents with regard to normal restriction of child behavior. Afraid of causing harmful inhibitions, they fail to place wholesome limitations on their children's demands for attention. Another cause may be the admiration which parents have for dynamic, out-going behavior. They believe sincerely that aggressiveness is essential for group recognition and therefore they encourage the child in this type of behavior.

A more frequent cause of aggressive behavior is that the child does not receive sufficient attention unless he demands it. This may be due to preoccupation of parents with their own lives, relative unattractiveness of the particular child as compared with other children in the family, or less frequently a rejection of the child by the parents because of their own emotional distress.

WAYS OF HELPING

All children who are too aggressive need to feel that the teacher recognizes their good qualities and approves of them even though their behavior must be curbed. Children who have never had limits placed on their behavior will learn what is expected of them by the restrictions placed on them by their classmates as well as by the teacher. As soon as they feel somewhat assured of the teacher's approval they will exercise self-control.

Children who are deprived of rightful attention at home adjust to classroom restrictions with greater difficulty. Very often these children have never known the interest of a sympathetic adult. Therefore they tend to regard with distrust any adult who shows a personal interest in them, and it takes a longer time for the teacher to convince them of her appreciation. The teacher should seek to give approval inconspicuously for any worth-while accomplishment and at the same time by careful planning she should avoid placing such children in situations that arouse aggressive responses. Any legitimate outlet for expression, such as dramatics, opportunity for leadership, or special tasks which are within their ability to handle, will help these children in learning to exercise control when necessary.

The Case of Marjorie

Marjorie entered the first grade and became conspicuous from the first day because she was larger than the other girls in the class, had a strident voice, and boundless energy. She soon had trouble with her classmates and the teacher. The children avoided her and excluded her from their games because she always wished to direct and would quarrel if they did not obey her. She seemed to the teacher to seek ways of annoying her.

Marjorie's home life was tempestuous. A younger sister, quite opposite in type from Marjorie, being small for her age and quiet, was enjoyed by the parents. Both father and mother worked in order to provide an adequate income. During their time at home they found it impossible to be patient with Marjorie's demands for attention and her persistent quarreling with her younger sister.

When Marjorie entered the third grade she met a teacher who was interested in gaining her cooperation. The teacher had studied Marjorie's record carefully. She recognized the child's high intellectual capacity and realized that her difficulty centered around her inability to gain social acceptance. She first challenged Marjorie's intellectual ability by giving her individual problems that would contribute to the class work. She gave her responsibilities that enabled them to work together. In so far as possible the child was directed toward social situations in which she could exercise self-control and thereby gain acceptance. In her conferences with the parents the teacher emphasized Marjorie's good points and helped the parents to accept her more readily. Though the difficulty at home was not solved through this procedure, the tension that Marjorie was feeling both at home and in school was decreased and Marjorie began many satisfactory social experiences.

SIGNIFICANCE OF WITHDRAWING BEHAVIOR

Children who tend to withdraw from classroom activity are far more in need of the teacher's consideration than aggressive children. These children usually appear timid or nondescript. Their thoughts, ideas, and feelings are completed within themselves and have no opportunity for reconstruction by contact with the thinking of the group. Frequently the thoughts and ideas of timid or nondescript children are very confused because they have been unable to obtain help from anyone in clarifying them. A lively imagination may often add to the difficulty.

UNDERLYING CAUSES

Timid or nondescript children have developed a mask or sphinxlike expression in order to protect themselves from unsympathetic adults. These children have found out early in life, usually by the third or fourth year of age, that the kinds of feelings they have and the responses they make spontaneously are disliked or ridiculed by members of the family. Survival demands that they protect the part of themselves that is disliked and at the same time give overt expression to the traits desired by their environment. Underneath the bland exterior usually evidenced, emotions are turbulent. These children surprise one often by violent outbursts of anger. The situation causing the anger outburst may be very slight but dammed up emotion bursts forth at a slight stimulus. These are the children who, if they start laughing, frequently are unable to stop. The need of release overpowers awareness of the situation. They also may sob uncontrollably at a very slight provocation when they have never been known to cry in this way before.

WAYS OF HELPING

Children who tend to withdraw need encouragement given inconspicuously. If conspicuous attention is given to them they feel that the mask they have adopted has been pierced. Thus threatened they will endeavor to withdraw further from contact with others. Inconspicuous approval should be given on the basis of work or product rather than on personal qualities. As soon as these children feel the teacher is respecting their reserve they will begin to respond personally to the approval that the teacher has shown. Their first outgoing feelings may be of great love and affection for the teacher. Even though their admiration takes on characteristics of a "crush," it is nevertheless wholesome, for love and admiration are outgoing feelings. The "crush" is a steppingstone only to feelings of friendliness for their classmates. Teachers may help children meet success in their first outgoing love responses by accepting but not prolonging them. If the crush is frowned upon, the first advance these children are attempting to make is thwarted. Their response is to return into their shell more completely than before.

Timid or nondescript children need an opportunity to succeed in individual work. Often the first awakening of self-confidence comes with the knowledge that they compete well with other children. If this is their only outlet, they may become single-tracked individuals interested only in accomplishment superior to that of their fellows. This creates one-sided development, usually in the intellectual field only, and ultimately results in unsatisfactory adjustment to life as other needs of the personality are denied. However, if academic achievement awakens self-confidence, the dangers of one-sided development may be offset through kindly encouragement of other interests.

In group units of work these children feel more comfortable when they are given special tasks rather than being allowed free rein to work out their own contribution. Relatively formalized work with specific directions until some mastery has been achieved is generally more conducive to development of these children than a free situation in which they are encouraged to be self-directive. These children are easily discouraged. It is essential, therefore, that standards of achievement be kept within their level of ability. It is more profitable for them to be the best in a group even though they may be older than to be placed in their own age group and be at the lower end of the scale.

The Case of Andrew

Andrew came into the first grade a quiet, unobtrusive, undemanding little boy. He watched the teacher closely and attempted to do all that was requested. He would struggle along on a piece of work even though his face became flushed, rather than ask help of anyone or admit that he did not know what to do. One day Andrew had been working quietly with a group of children while the teacher was busy with another group. Suddenly there were loud wails and, to the teacher's amazement, she saw Andrew sobbing violently. She immediately asked the children around him if anyone had hurt Andrew. Their expressions seemed to prove their innocence so she tried to find out from Andrew what the matter was. He made a tremendous effort to stop crying, only to burst out again. The teacher was unable to get any coherent remark from him to indicate the cause. She finally decided to leave Andrew alone and drew the interest of the other children away from him. In a conference later with the mother she found that Andrew frequently had crying spells when no particular cause could be found.

Andrew was observed more closely. The teacher discovered that he seldom made spontaneous remarks. He showed tension by the rigid way in which he held his body and by nervous twitching of his fingers. Through the parents' help, standards for Andrew at home and school were lowered. Inconspicuous approval was given for any gesture Andrew made toward independent action even if it violated classroom rules. Andrew gradually began to experiment with more daring actions. At the end of the year he was becoming obnoxious because he was relaxing so completely and had no understanding of how to control spontaneous behavior. He had a great deal of ground to cover because for six years he had been inactive. It was necessary for parents and teacher to show Andrew the limits in behavior he must accept, and at the same time indicate their approval of hi' wide-awake interest in life.

SIGNIFICANCE OF TEASING

Teasing is a very revealing behavior, whether the person be the teaser or the one being teased. Children, as we have said previously, need a feeling of power or prestige in a group. There is no easier way to secure a feeling of power than to be a successful teaser. Because children respond to other human beings on an intuitive, emotional basis, they often sense in other children and adults vulnerable points that pass unnoticed by the casual observer. The child who is successful in teasing always touches the vulnerable point in the person he teases. Teasers seldom select a child who will ignore the teasing, but always one who will show a response. Teasers are always children who seek a short way to power. This is a pattern of behavior that will handicap a child if he continues to use it and will result in isolation from the group.

Children who are recipients of teasing are always those who lack self-confidence. Sometimes the point at which they are vulnerable seems insignificant to the adult, but if we observe carefully, we gain insight into the aspects of the child's personality of which he feels uncertain. These may include size, clothes, ability, family background, language, personal habits, or any other projection of the personality. Though these points may appear insignificant to the adult, all help should be given to children to protect the area that disturbs them. Sometimes it is not possible to eliminate the difficulties, and the approach has to be through understanding. The points at which children are teased are always characteristics that distinguish them from the group.

1. Are there some children in your class who are using teasing as a source of power? Can you find a more constructive way for them to secure prestige?
2. Are there some children who are easy targets for teasing?
3. Note the methods used by teasers and the methods of defense used by children being teased.

RESPONSE TO INTERFERENCE OR THWARTING

Interference or thwarting may occur in response to frustration with materials, as a result of teacher direction that interferes with activity, or because of interference by other children.

Frustration with materials represents to the child a problem situation. It has been noted above that the response to problem solving is a pattern of behavior that is developed early. In watching a child when he strikes a snag in working with wood, with paints, in attempting to write, or in any of the many manual skills, the teacher should look for the following:

1. Does he mobilize his abilities and attempt a fresh attack upon the problem?
2. Does he give up and turn to some other more satisfactory material?
3. Does he use a haphazard trial-and-error attack?
4. Does he consider carefully a new plan of attack?

When teacher direction interferes with an activity we have not only the frustration created by the interference, but a personal-social reaction against the adult. A child, in fact, may not object seriously to the interference of the teacher as far as the work he is doing is concerned, but the adult authority

evidenced may cause a resistant response. He may accept interference from adults in any of the following ways:

1. He may accept the interference even though he resents it.
2. He may protest violently or refuse to obey.
3. He may appear to accept as long as he is under the scrutiny
   of the teacher and then pursue his former plans as soon as
   the teacher's attention is directed elsewhere.
4. He may accept the teacher's direction, but carry it out in
   a lackadaisical manner.

Children's response to interference by other children involves
personal-social relations. If the child who is interfering is
friendly, the response from other children is usually cooperative. If the child is one who makes trouble, children will com-
bat the interference first with words and then with blows. By
the upper elementary school age, children have learned many
tactics for getting around interference by other children.

1. Which children in your class are most adroit in resisting interference
   by other children? What methods do they use? Are these methods
   socially acceptable?
2. Are some children so considerate of others that they have little time to
   attend to their own work?
3. Do some children accept interference in their work as a relief and
   thus become completely diverted from the task at hand?

THE ROLE OF THE TEACHER

THE TEACHER AS AN ALLY AND MENTOR

The teacher plays an influential part in the life of every child
during the first few years of his school life. She inducts children of the primary school into a new realm of activity, one
which has great import for them because of the value placed on
success in school by the majority of homes and communities.
A child of this age responds quickly to kindliness, and all efforts
on the part of the teacher to place herself as his ally, working
with him to meet the requirements of the school situation, receive a wholehearted response.

In the upper elementary school, children need the teacher as an ally and mentor but hesitate to show that they wish such a relationship. Experience has shown them that dependence on the teacher is not accepted. They want a certain degree of independence, but feel much happier if they can rely on an adult to help them over the more difficult phases of living. The teacher who is able to establish a relationship of working with these children has a valuable influence that cannot be measured by improvement in classroom accomplishment. Experiencing an understanding relationship with an adult gives children a concept of friendliness that is of permanent value in their lives.

1. Which children in your classroom do you find it possible to work with—figuratively walking hand in hand with them?
2. Are there situations in which you find yourself pulling the class along or even working at cross purposes?
3. Are there situations in which you feel yourself working with the entire class, guiding them as an adult mentor but also as an ally in helping them to move toward a goal?

RELATIONSHIP OF CHILDREN AND TEACHER

Children change in the relationship they expect with a teacher as they proceed from kindergarten through the grades. When they first enter school, being familiar with the parental role and unfamiliar with the teacher role, they regard the teacher as a substitute parent. The teacher is a person to please if possible. Self-confidence shows visible growth when the teacher approves; lack of success in securing the teacher's approval creates lack of confidence. As little children live in the present, a day when approval is lacking is a gray day. A teacher may observe the children's response to her by noting the difference in their behavior when she is in the mood to find the class interesting and responsive. Even the children who have been recalcitrant in their behavior begin to show interest in meeting the requirements.

1. Have you observed that some children are able to change their tactics to secure approval as they sense that your mood has set different requirements?

2. Are some children increasing their resistance as discipline becomes more necessary? Do they show that they have given up hope of securing your approval?

3. Are some children putting their utter faith in you as a mother substitute and securing protection in return?

4. Do some children need your attention and approval so much that they try one thing after another to get it?

Children in the upper elementary grades usually have outgrown a substitute parent-child relationship. They are beginning to meet all personal-social relationships with a discerning eye. They have had enough experience with teachers by this time to realize that they differ from one another. They have had enough experience with authority to realize that commands may be ignored and that cooperation is *given* by them, not *demanded* of them. Their development of group loyalty with their fellow classmates gives them the strength of many like-minded souls to resist if the teacher is unjust.

These children differ from younger children in another respect. They are able to pay passing heed to the present. If the teacher has proved her interest in them and also her fairness, they are able to overlook minor infringements of these attributes on the part of the teacher. Pleasantness and unpleasantness can be accepted from adults without undue concern because they are no longer emotionally dependent upon them.

1. Have you noticed in children in the fifth, sixth, or seventh grade a spontaneous response of enthusiasm when a light or humorous touch is brought into an erstwhile listless period?

2. Have you noticed side glances at you or at one another when your enthusiasm for achievement sets an impossible standard?

3. Is there a concerted plan to get you started on a favorite topic that they can enjoy with you?

4. Have a few children let you in on a secret after a particularly happy period together?

THE TEACHER AS A SYMBOL OF AUTHORITY

By the time children enter kindergarten they have already a pattern of behavior toward adults in authority. They may show perfect freedom in talking with adults, accepting them as kindly persons who are willing to share their interests. They may regard adults as formidable persons who should be avoided, or as cruel persons who are given authority in order to interfere with children's pleasures. An attitude of distrust toward adults is regarded as unfortunate, because it means that children are going to have to learn how to live in an extremely complex world with little guidance from mature persons. If this attitude continues during the upper elementary and junior high school age, children are burdened with the necessity of working things out as best they can either alone or with the help of equally confused friends.

Responsibility for changing attitudes toward adults rests upon the teacher in the primary grades. To the child she exemplifies authority. If she can gain the confidence of those children who regard her as formidable or cruel because she represents authority, she will prepare them for receiving help from adults willingly. The teacher in the upper elementary grades should stand in the role of a friendly adviser. As children learn to trust authority, there is a natural transition from the mother substitute role desired from the primary teacher to acceptance of the friendly adviser relationship of the upper elementary school teacher. One may detect in the spontaneous conversations of children the attitude which they have toward the teacher.

1. Which children in your class talk with you spontaneously? What is the nature of their conversation or confidences?
2. Are there some children who watch you shyly but never venture a direct remark?
3. Are there some children who avoid you and act defiantly whenever your back is turned?
4. Do you have children who have a frightened look whenever you approach them directly?

RELATION OF TEACHER APPROVAL
TO COMPETITION

While modern education seeks to minimize competition, it exists in school work for two reasons: first, the teacher's approval sets a standard which most children attempt to reach;

second, it is only through observation of what other children do that a child can get an idea of his own abilities.

Throughout their earlier school years, children are trying to find out what they are like. A great part of the image or picture they build up of themselves is in terms of what they can do, based on teacher approval. This may be noted in any classroom. As spelling papers or compositions are returned in class, children will look carefully at one another's and decide which is best. If the papers are graded, children may determine quickly the relative worth of their work. When no grade is placed on papers returned more time is required to compare their work with others, but compare it they will. If you ask any child above the second grade about the ranking of other children, he will be able to tell you with remarkable accuracy. Unawareness of the group's rankings may be regarded as a defense technique used by children who are fearful of recognizing their limitations.

Many schools are attempting to eliminate competition between children. However, when competition is wisely handled it helps children gain an accurate estimate of their abilities and limitations. No more valuable service can be performed by teachers in elementary schools than to help children develop a self-esteem that is realistic. A child's awareness of his *growth* as well as his achievement helps him to set standards for himself. This is sometimes called competition with the self. Even though this be the predominant method used, the fact that children are working in a group with other children and that their work is being judged makes competition inevitable. Rather than ignore the fact that it exists, we must utilize competition to forward children's growth.

1. Which children feel the necessity of being in advance of the group? This indicates again a need for power and assurance.
2. What methods do children use to accomplish high ranking?
3. Which children seem unaware of the achievement of other members of the group?
4. Are there some children who work hard but never succeed in commanding respect from the group?

SUMMARY

How to study the behavior of children has been discussed in this chapter under three general points, namely, the value of observing behavior by means of samples that may be part of the child's cumulative record; checking each child's physical, intellectual, social, and emotional development in order to determine his relative growth in these areas; and lastly the role the teacher may take with individual children in meeting their needs in adult-child relationships. In the discussions of these three approaches to the study of children's behavior clues have been suggested to help the teacher find the causes motivating the child's responses. In the following chapter suggestions will be given for using the knowledge gained to direct the behavior of children into constructive outlets through satisfaction of their needs. As soon as a teacher is able to understand causes of behavior and direct her classroom activities and relationships toward meeting children's needs as indicated by the causes, classroom activities become a constructive experience both for children and for teacher.

CHAPTER THREE

Using Knowledge of Children's Behavior

AFTER facts concerning behavior in classroom situations have been obtained through observation, the question always arises what shall be done with this knowledge? Many weary hours are spent in gathering records and putting them on cards. Unless this information is used by the teacher to help the children in her class, the time and energy expended on the records are wasted. Records are of value only in terms of their usability. If their use is not demonstrated within a short time, the procedure should be reorganized and only those records kept that are of value.

The role of the teacher as outlined in the preceding chapters pictures her as an understanding mature human interested primarily in the growth needs of the children in her class. Teaching techniques will be evolved, therefore, not from particular subject matter but from the growth needs of individual children and the interrelationships existing in the classroom. This teacher "is alive to the child's human relationships. She knows when to bolster up the family discipline and when to encourage emancipation, when to follow through if something is not going well and when to attempt new assignment, when to show an objective interest in a pupil and when to express a personal feeling."[1]

In this chapter suggestions will be made for utilizing knowledge of the growth needs of individual children. Emphasis will be placed on methods that may be used with children and with

[1] Patey, Henry C. "The Teacher as a General Practitioner in Mental Hygiene." *Mental Hygiene*, 24:600-613, October, 1940.

parents. Suggestions for utilizing community resources will also be given.

CHILDREN'S ASSETS AND LIABILITIES

VALUE OF USING CHILDREN'S STRONGEST AREA OF ACCOMPLISHMENT

Children function at their best when they work in their strongest area of accomplishment, that is, in the area where they have the greatest feeling of competence. Interest is high, thought flows more easily, ingenuity is stimulated. Even under these circumstances, however, level of achievement may fall far short of the child's ability. Work habits may be slovenly and interest may be concerned solely with achieving a goal as rapidly as possible. However, the fact that the child is interested gives the teacher an opportunity to help him achieve results that will be gratifying to him. Assistance in planning, in improving a weak point in technique, in giving a polish to the final product will provide standards of work that are meaningful.

FOR IMPROVEMENT OF CHILDREN'S SKILLS AND HABITS OF WORK

When an erstwhile resistant child is working in an area of competence, a teacher may approach him and thus begin to establish a much more satisfactory relationship. Because a child's emotional tone is likely to be more optimistic when he is working in his strongest area of accomplishment, a teacher may give suggestions on method of work and standards that would be resisted or pass unnoticed if he were working with less confidence. The only caution necessary here is to beware of pressing a point or interfering to the extent of detracting from the child's interest and enthusiasm. It is necessary to move slowly and to work with the child—not direct his procedure. It is sometimes desirable to leave a child completely alone so that he may have the supreme satisfaction of carrying through something in the area of competence under his own direction.

1. Observe the area of work in which a child seems to be most expansive, enthusiastic, and spontaneous. This is probably his area of greatest competence, even though he may at the moment achieve little.

2. Watch the child's work habits, the standards he holds for himself, and the relations he seeks with the teacher and other children when working with enthusiasm and confidence.

3. See how ready the child is to improve his skills when working in an area of competence. If he is having a struggle with other work, it will be unwise to emphasize work habits in his one satisfying experience.

4. See what groupings may be made with children in the class who have the same area of interest and competence. This is sometimes the best way in which to include a child who seems on the outside of group activities.

FOR DEVELOPING GREATER SELF-CONFIDENCE

Opportunity to work in an area in which he has ability should increase a child's self-confidence. This does not always follow, however. Children frequently underrate their abilities and lack the confidence in their work that should naturally follow the ability they show. Basic to the development of self-confidence is an attitude of realistic self-assurance which the teacher may help children to achieve through her comments on the work. The teacher should reassure honestly on the points where the child shows ability. Where marks are not used, a definite statement should be made after work has been completed that will enable the child to evaluate both the procedure and product of his effort. This is done by pointing out the strong points in the work and omitting mention of the weak points. The time will come when the weaker points may be mentioned. Though perhaps not admitting it to themselves children usually are aware of places where their work has failed to measure up to standard. In other words, the teacher guides, and aims to give a feeling of satisfaction and pride in that part of the work honestly performed at the highest level of which a child is capable.

1. Observe the aspect of work which seems most gratifying to the child.
2. Also observe the doubts and uncertainties which the child expresses

by facial expression, gestures, and, in some rare instances, words. Try to find some point connected with his work on which you may give sincere praise.

3. Watch carefully those children who boast of their competence. They are usually in need of reassurance.

FOR SHOWING STRENGTH THAT MAY BE USED IN AREAS OF DIFFICULTY

Work in an area of competence usually utilizes abilities which children might use in areas of difficulty. Frequently they show aptitudes and skills when working in an area of competence that are never utilized at other times. They may develop a sound plan for approach in an area of competence; in an area of difficulty their approach may be haphazard or by trial and error. Children eight years of age and older may be able to visualize the approach that they are utilizing when working at their best. If they are unable to transfer this plan when working in an area of difficulty, it denotes at once that fear in regard to the difficulty has blocked their ability to think. One may then see the cause of the difficulty and work on fear rather than on specific skills.

It is most characteristic, however, for children to fail to see the similarity between ability used in an area of competence and ability required in an area of difficulty. Analysis of the identity of the skills used in the two areas may bring about the first awareness of similarities in the situations. In this way a teacher may utilize a child's assets for attack upon difficulties.

1. Analyze the overlapping abilities that are used by children in the various tasks they are required to do.
2. Watch those children who show the greatest discrepancy between accomplishment in the area of competence and in the area of difficulty. Try to find the most significant skill used in the area of competence that is not used as well in the area of difficulty.

FOR GAINING ASCENDANCE OR PRESTIGE IN ONE AREA OF SCHOOL WORK

Competitive groupings require that individuals in the group have one area at least in which they have prestige because of an acceptable contribution. As elementary schools expand their programs to include a variety of activities, more opportunity is given for children to find areas in which they are particularly capable. A teacher who is sensitive to the growth needs of children is able to manipulate the situation so that each child can have opportunity for expression of his abilities. This may be done by arranging groups on the basis of interest and ability, and placing the children who have one outstanding ability in a dominant position in the group. Other children, equally competent, may be shifted to a second interest group in which they will not threaten the self-confidence of the less able children.

The Case of Edward

Edward was a boy in the fifth grade who was fortunate in having a teacher who recognized the value of working through the area of confidence in helping him overcome his uncertainty in other areas. Edward was very capable intellectually and very conscientious in preparing his work. He worked alone almost entirely and was isolated from the other boys in all their spontaneous activity. Though recognized in the classroom as capable, he was never sought by the other boys for help either in classroom work or playtime activities. The teacher recognized in this child a capable and, at the same time, tolerant person. She believed that he would be able to manage leadership in classroom work without being smug. She therefore appointed him chairman in a social studies unit that required considerable library work. The teacher helped the group organize and had Edward suggest the books in the library that would be most helpful in the unit of work. During the entire unit, Edward was sought frequently by other children. He began to realize through this and other experiences that he was not only capable but could transfer some of his abilities from intellectual satisfactions to social satisfactions. By some miracle, the children chose him spontaneously for captain of a team in running a race. Edward used every ounce of his strength in running and, because of his endeavor, made a good showing. The teacher could never analyze how it happened that Edward was chosen leader of the team. These miracles do happen in schools. The significant point is that Edward was able to live up to the honor given to him. Gradually one would see Edward working with groups and less often working alone. Even when working on an individual project he was not isolated from the class. It is rather unusual that prestige in academic work carries over so successfully to the non-academic work, but starting with the area of competence was the step that enabled the children to recognize Edward's ability.

Gaining ascendance or prestige does not necessarily mean that the child's abilities are flaunted before the class. This frequently causes more embarrassment than satisfaction to sensitive children. Given an opportunity to work with success in a group is reassuring in itself. A child will derive greater satisfaction in gaining the spontaneous approval of other children than in securing overt teacher approval.

1. Have you discovered the area in which each child does his best work?
2. Has each child had an opportunity to receive recognition from a worth-while contribution?
3. Have you found opportunity for a child to gain prestige by contributing in his area of greatest accomplishment?

CAUSES OF FAILURE

The approach of the teacher should vary according to the cause of failure. Causes of failure are manifold. It has been stated previously that fear of attack on the subject is a primary cause of failure. Self-distrust because of high standards put before the child is another dominant cause. Other causes are failure to understand the basic intellectual process because of lack of readiness at the time the material was first presented, disability in a particular subject due to physiological or intellectual deviations, resistance to adults who impose particular subject matter, or distraction resulting from inner conflicts.

FEAR OF FAILURE

Fear of failure in an activity that is required distorts the difficulty of the task before the child. The requirements loom as a hurdle that cannot be surmounted. In consequence, these children avoid facing the task directly, just as a horse that has become fearful of a jump will stop short in front of it. The fear may not lie in inability to do the task, but in emotional intangibles that have become associated with it. The teacher may help these children by giving them intermediate steps in reaching the goal so that they really move by easy stages. Specific directions on the first step in the process and subsequent suggestions may enable them to accomplish the task successfully. One success under these conditions is not enough to overcome the fear, and it will be necessary for the teacher to help step by step, time and time again. One would expect that if a teacher helped with five steps one day, perhaps she might have to help with only four the next and three the next. As it actually works out, it may be necessary for the teacher to help with all five steps for several days and then to help with only two steps. When they have gained confidence, children may jump quickly to independent work, but until then, all the help needed must be given.

1. Have you noticed some children who seem overwhelmed by the task required of them?
2. Have you tried giving help sympathetically and inconspicuously to children who are having difficulty?
3. Have you started giving as much help as a child needs and contributing this help until he gives evidence of greater assurance in attacking the work?
4. Have you tried limiting assignments within each child's persistence and ability level?

SELF-DISTRUST DUE TO TOO HIGH STANDARDS

Self-distrust is closely associated with the fear of failure, but the specific condition of self-distrust may be the high standards held up to the child by parents and teacher. The child is afraid to proceed through the natural learning stages. He believes that he must approach an "A" standard at once, when in reality a new task may start on a much lower level of achievement. It is often advisable to work with the child's parents in order to establish standards within the child's ability that are mutually satisfactory to the parents and the teacher.

We often see self-distrust operating when children first begin to read. Older brothers and sisters may have much more important looking books. The parents may have in mind a first reader, and instead the child must start with preprimer material or small, individual booklets. To many parents it seems humorous to characterize as reading the work with these books, and so they view the child's effort with amusement. They tell others that their little child really thinks he is reading. As a result the child feels that unless he has a real book at once, he is failing in his parents' eyes.

1. Have some children in your class asked for "harder work"? This usually is a reflection of home standards and indicates that parents do not comprehend the standards being held by the teacher.
2. Have any of your children shown embarrassment or a derogatory attitude toward their level of accomplishment?
3. Do some children seem indifferent to their successes?

LACK OF READINESS

Every teacher is familiar with the children who are not ready for the work of a particular grade in which they are placed by age and mental ability. These children operate under a definite handicap, whether it be intellectual, emotional, or social lack of readiness. Until the cause of the lack of readiness is discovered, it is foolhardy to have the child attempt the work. On the other hand, it is not advisable to ignore the situation and hope that time will solve the difficulty.

We have learned how to meet intellectual lack of readiness through analysis of the cause. Diagnostic tests help to isolate the cause and enable the teacher to proceed on a systematic basis to correct the difficulty. Social or emotional lack of readiness presents a very different problem. We have few available tests to isolate the difficulty, and when the cause is found the teacher is baffled because of lack of training in how to proceed. Help must be sought from the home for minor causes and from the specialist in more serious cases. (See page 77.)

1. Do some children in your class show lack of readiness for the work?
2. Have you carefully analyzed possible causes of the difficulty?
3. Have you tried a systematic approach to eliminate the difficulty? If no success is secured in your approach, have you attempted further analysis of the cause or of your method of approach?

PHYSIOLOGICAL OR INTELLECTUAL DEVIATION

Physiological or intellectual deviation below the average of the group is a definite handicap. The most common difficulties are lower intelligence, left-handedness that may affect the reading and writing abilities of children, eye fusion that creates eyestrain when the child focuses on small symbols such as words and numbers and malnutrition that lowers energy and creates chronic fatigue. Each of these deviations requires special treatment. These children cannot progress at the rate or with the intensity characteristic of others in the class. When presented with material too difficult to understand or if required to work for longer periods than their physiological mechanism will permit, they fail to accomplish the required tasks. We then have coupled with the initial difficulty, chagrin caused by failure.

1. Are there children in your class who are developing a feeling of defeat because of a definite handicap that prevents them from doing the work?
2. Have you thought of all possible avenues for obtaining help in alleviating the situation?
3. Have you utilized inter-class groupings for minimizing the sense of defeat these children are developing?

RESISTANCE TO ADULTS

Some children enter the first grade after unfortunate experiences with adults. They have been subjected to continued restriction and in their effort to cope with the situation they frequently resort to revolt. Because revolt causes isolation from adults, these children usually are unhappy and feel they are unworthy of commendation. The teacher, as another adult, is regarded with apprehension and the whole nervous system is set for resistance. Instead of being focused on learning their attention is focused on maintaining individuality and on holding their own against the adult. Not until the teacher has proved to these children that she is just, fair, and to be trusted will there be much evidence of accomplishment.

1. Have you tried methods of approval and reassurance with children who are resistant?
2. Can you find some activity in which these resistant children can be themselves and also gain your approval?

INNER CONFLICT

Much has already been said about the effect of inner conflicts upon the ability of the child to attend to matters relatively
superficial to him, such as classroom work. Solution of the inner
conflict is paramount, and all available energy, attention, and
persistence is directed toward this solution. These children
are often called lazy, indifferent, or phlegmatic. Behind each
one of these symptoms is a definite cause. Until a solution is
found, it is useless to expect achievement commensurate with
ability.

1. Are there some children in your class who daydream to such an extent
   that they scarcely know what is going on around them? These children are frequently turning to pleasant thoughts in order to forget
   the unpleasantness of life around them.
2. Do some children bite their nails, suck thumb or finger, or masturbate
   at the time they are daydreaming? Sensory stimulation seems to give
   reassurance to these children.
3. Do some children appear listless and uninterested in their work?

SIGNIFICANCE OF METHODS USED IN GIVING APPROVAL

Most people, both children and adults, accept reassurance
from a person in authority, but individuals differ in the kind
of reassurance that is pleasing to them. Reassurance may be
direct or indirect; on the work that the person has done or
on the kind of person he is. It may be conspicuous or inconspicuous.

Direct reassurance on one's work is acceptable to almost
everyone. Attention given in this way does not create self-consciousness because it is on the product rather than the person
himself. Direct approval of work has to be sincere, otherwise
one who is capable of honest self-evaluation will lose trust
in the person giving the reassurance. So often we say in a
kindly tone that such a piece of work is good, or fine. In the
child's own estimation it may have many shortcomings, and
so the reassurance serves only to lower the teacher in his eyes.

Direct praise of personal qualities, even though connected with the work, is of questionable value. This draws attention to the child himself and frequently creates self-consciousness and embarrassment. Also, if this is the type of reassurance that gives pleasure, there is evidence of smugness and increased egocentricity.

Conspicuous approval is the method used most frequently in classrooms. Children's work is cited and praised before the entire class, often quite lavishly. This method is used because it helps to set for all children in the class the standard desired by the teacher. If used to any extent, however, it is destructive of class morale. It frequently is hard on the children receiving the approval because the other children become jealous. The teacher's "pet" is never in an enviable position. He may bask in the teacher's approval but he loses out in his relations with his classmates because he is set above them. It is much safer to discuss the good points of several pieces of work, thus setting the standard without isolating one child's work for marked approval.

Indirect approval is usually satisfying to retiring or timid children. It may be given, not by drawing attention to something well done, but by appointing a child to an office, or sending him on a special errand shortly after the successful performance. These children sense the approval and are reassured by the confidence shown in them. Almost inevitably they are aware of the connection between the task well done and the special privilege allowed.

Inconspicuous approval may be given by dropping a remark to a child as one passes or by a quick smile of recognition for work done. With some children even this sort of approval is embarrassing because it is personal. Until the teacher has the confidence of the child a mark of approval may be given by commenting "well done," using a particular check that means the work is excellent, or putting a special piece of work in the teacher's drawer for safekeeping. Many children are so in need of approval that if it is given conspicuously it makes them self-conscious, or elated to a degree that is uncontrollable. Surprised at receiving adult approval, they are thrown into an exultation that they are unable to manage. This is particularly true if by some miracle a child who has not done anything well finally turns in a good piece of work. Any tendency these children may have toward uncontrolled behavior is let loose by their strong emotional response to unexpected approval. As soon as these children gain confidence in the teacher and achieve success in their work, they are able to respond without embarrassment to more direct approval.

1. Are there some children in your class who are dangerously near isolation from the group because of their marked success in gaining teacher approval?
2. Are there some children you dare not praise because they become impossible to manage after receiving approbation?
3. Have you tried to develop inconspicuous methods of showing approval?

VALUE OF FLEXIBLE GROUPING

Children who feel incompetent or who are failing frequently feel lost when working with an entire class group. Tensions may be reduced and greater confidence developed if small groups are used. As was pointed out previously, if a child has a particular friend in a group and feels confidence in the presence of that friend, being placed in the same group will decrease tension. Such groups may be closely related to ability groups in that children are placed with classmates working on the same level of material. In this way they are not overwhelmed by the greater accomplishment of other members of the class. Often a good way to set up a group is to study friendships, watch those children who do not overpower others, and, in forming groups, place the child who feels incompetent with the predominantly gentle group. Shifting groups frequently for various kinds of work is probably one of the most useful ways of developing assurance. Flexible grouping enables a teacher to help children assume their place in the class by a series of successful experiences and therefore presages greater self-confidence in dealing with life situations.

The Case of Betty

Betty was a child in the fourth grade who was having difficulty with arithmetic. She was an extremely attractive girl, whose face brightened with laughter easily but who became sober when the arithmetic work period was in progress. She had managed for the three years previously to do passable work in arithmetic. In the fourth grade, however, her lack of understanding prevented any success. When help was given Betty it was found that her mother never could do arithmetic, that ladies did not have to do arithmetic, that girls were essentially supposed to be attractive and happy. If you cried over arithmetic you were not pretty, so your father, mother, or teacher would help you.

Betty was shown how quick she was in playing number games, how accurate her eye was in approximating distances. She was reassured again and again of her fundamental aptitude in dealing with number concepts. She was shown the number of girls in the school who could do arithmetic and who enjoyed doing it. Simple problems were given in brief periods of work. The work was attacked seriously and successful achievement was made possible. Frequent tests of three or four examples showed Betty how much she had learned. She made her own chart of progress. At the latest report Betty is having no difficulty in arithmetic.

USING SCHOOL SPECIALISTS AND COMMUNITY AGENCIES

Teachers are general practitioners[2] in the area of guidance. In any type of professional work the general practitioner finds himself limited when special cases come to him. The teacher is in the same position. There will appear in her class from time to time children who are so disturbed that they are unable to profit from group experiences. All the patience and understanding in the world will not enable the teacher to help these children. Time will not solve the problem. The teacher then must seek a specialist to help her.

In any school system or community there are people who by training and interest are capable of working with disturbed children. They are specialists usually affiliated with some educational or community agency. Many school psychologists and school nurses have training in child guidance. More and

[2] Patey, Henry C. "The Teacher as a General Practitioner in Mental Hygiene." *Mental Hygiene,* 24:600-613, October 1940.

more staff members of churches are specializing in psychological counseling and child guidance work. Social workers in child welfare agencies or in community organizations are trained in this field. Truant officers are being selected more frequently from the field of social work. Boys' Clubs, Girl Scouts, Y. M. C. A. and Y. W. C. A., and Rotary Clubs often have on their staffs people trained in counseling. Instead of worrying about the child and pushing one's patience to the limit, the teacher should canvass the community for someone to help this particular child. This does not indicate failure on the part of the teacher but an awareness of the limitation that her professional preparation has placed upon her. She should feel adequate if she can take care of 95 per cent of the children.

1. Do you know the specialists in your school? Try to know them through discussion of less serious behavior problems.
2. Do you know the work being done by community agencies, particularly child welfare agencies?
3. Have you tried to find out the work being done by the truant officer? Even if he cannot give you direct help he can give you a great deal of information about the homes from which these children come.
4. Investigate the work your own church is doing in providing opportunities for working individually with parents or children.

CUMULATIVE SCHOOL RECORDS

Cumulative records form an essential part of an educational program that has as its aim the growth of individual pupils. They should include basic information that will help each teacher to understand home and neighborhood conditions, techniques used by former teachers, and the personality characteristics that will indicate the most constructive approach to be used with each child.

Discussions often arise concerning the relative value of cumulative records. Many teachers feel that they may become biased if they read a complete record of a child before knowing him thoroughly. They feel that a child gains a reputation that is difficult to modify if detailed records are kept each year. It is true that if one views behavior as unchangeable, cumulative records may set a child's pattern so that each teacher inadvertently attempts to keep the child in the same pattern rather than giving him an opportunity to change to a more desirable one. Even though this danger exists, cumulative records have a definite contribution. Frequently a pattern of behavior is not understood, even though the teacher may try her utmost to comprehend its cause. When, however, one reads a cumulative sample of a child's behavior over a two- or three-year period, the repetition of particular behavior may furnish a clue to the fundamental cause underlying the whole pattern of the child's responses.

VARIATION IN RECORDS USED

As one would expect, there is wide variation in the types of cumulative records and home reports used by elementary public schools. Some schools still retain a cumulative record that reports the pupil's name, date of birth, address and telephone number and guardian's name and address and telephone number, grades in academic achievement, and some notation of results of mental tests and achievement tests. Other schools have moved away from this type of cumulative record and include items on home and family background, description of achievement rather than grades, abilities and interests of pupils as observed by teachers and parents, physical condition and health, growth record including growth and health, social and work habits, skills and interests. The record also includes reports of findings on mental and educational tests. Among the many school systems using the latter type of records are Bronxville, N. Y., and Los Angeles and Pasadena, Calif.

RECORD OF HOME AND FAMILY BACKGROUND

When the cumulative record contains a report on the home and family background, it usually includes names of both parents (mother's maiden name), address, occupation, information regarding the marital status—whether living together, separated, or divorced—number of brothers and sisters. and other people living in the home. Sometimes it includes a description of the physical properties of the home in relation to the needs of children, such as adequate space for living, play space, and general setup. All this information is pertinent. The general information regarding the parents serves mainly as identification, though reports on marital status give insight into the adjustment that a child has to make, particularly if the parents are separated or divorced, or have remarried. Usually the information on various people living in the home is too general to give any aid in understanding the situation with which the children have to cope. A fairly accurate picture of the physical properties of the home may be formed from the address alone if the teacher is familiar with the community.

The writer recommends additional information, some of which might be substituted for the more general information noted above. Information regarding the parents might include the approximate ages of both parents, educational background, and religious affiliation. This information is pertinent because it gives an idea of the areas of adjustment that have to be faced by the two parents. Generally, two individuals are able to make an adjustment in one area of their living; therefore difference in any one of the three areas would be of little significance. If, however, adjustment is required in all three areas, it serves to complicate the personal relationships between the parents.

The general information usually obtained concerning the children in the home does not give the teacher a clear idea of the situation with which the individual child in the family has to cope. It is not the number of children in the family that is significant, but the relative position in relation to age and sex of the child being studied. It is therefore advisable to have information regarding the age, sex, and grade placement of the individual children in the family.

REPORTS TO PARENTS

The newer types of report to parents of their children's progress in school differ in both form and content from the traditional report card.[3] Many schools send an informal letter periodically to parents of children in the primary grades. They are sent usually at the end of each semester though sometimes more frequently. Conferences between parents and teacher may be held at the time the letter is sent or at more frequent intervals if desired by either the teacher or the parents. By these means the parents are kept informed of their child's intellectual and social adjustment to school, his progress in academic achievement, and the results of physical examination. Emphasis is placed on the ability that the child has in organization of work, persistence, standards that he holds for his work, cooperativeness with classmates and teacher, and other personal characteristics conducive to individual growth and cooperative living.

Reports to parents of children's progress in the upper elementary school are usually more formal. They consist of ratings in academic subjects through descriptive terms such as very good, good, satisfactory, and unsatisfactory, and comments or ratings on various work habits and social characteristics. These reports are sent usually four times during the school year. Though parent-teacher conferences are held less frequently than with parents of primary children, either parents or teacher may request a conference if desired.

SUMMARY

In the preceding pages, the teacher's role in the education of elementary school children has been visualized as one in which the teacher seeks through her understanding of behavior to provide opportunities for growth and development. Under these circumstances education would consist of planning experiences that would give children a feeling of satisfaction in work accomplished. Each child would take sequential steps in physical, mental, emotional, and social learning as he is ready for

[3] Reports to parents used by Lincoln School and Horace Mann School of Teachers College, Columbia University, and those used by the elementary public schools of Pasadena, California, may be of particular interest to the reader.

them. Personal-social learnings would form the core of the curriculum. Education would be confined neither to so-called traditional methods nor to progressive methods. Some children may need clearly defined tasks that are set by the teacher, with outlets provided for response to aesthetic experiences. As these children begin to feel greater self-confidence, less specific requirements may be given to them and they may be encouraged toward creative expression. Other children in the same class may have matured emotionally to the point where they could be self-directive in many activities. The teacher acting as adviser should help them set limits for their work and behavior.

Recognition has been given throughout this discussion to the basic requirements of all children for status or recognition, for approval from teachers and other children, and for opportunity to advance in all areas of growth. School experiences are regarded as setting conditions for growth. They therefore cease to be ends in themselves but serve their purpose only as they provide the best means of growth for a particular group of children. Always to be kept in mind is the fact that children must grow toward a feeling of competence in dealing with the world in which they live. An idealistic plan of education that considers only children's individual needs would defeat its own goal. For this reason our American tradition of educating children in groups is basically sound. We need only to become more aware of individual members in the group.

There are no set rules for pursuing this sort of education. Through understanding of human behavior on the one hand, and understanding of our culture on the other, the teacher must continually evaluate her procedures to enable children to move forward with realistic self-assurance.

Bibliography

Anderson, Harold H. *Children in the Family*. New York, D. Appleton-Century Company, 1937. xii+253 p.

Bailey, E. W., Laton, A. D., and Bishop, E. L. *Studying Children in School*. Second Edition. New York, McGraw-Hill Book Company, 1939. vii+182 p.

Baruch, Dorothy. *Parents and Children Go to School*. Chicago, Scott, Foresman and Company, 1939. xiv+504 p.

Bridges, K. M. *Social and Emotional Development of the Pre-school Child*. London, Kegan Paul, 1931. 277 p.

Brooks, F. D. *Child Psychology*. Boston, Houghton Mifflin Company, 1937. xxx+600 p.

Brown, F. J. *The Sociology of Childhood*. New York, Prentice-Hall, 1939. 498 p.

De Schweinitz, Karl. *Growing Up*. Second Edition Revised. New York, The Macmillan Company, 1935. 95 p.

Goodenough, Florence. *Developmental Psychology*. New York, D. Appleton-Century Company, 1934. 619 p.

Heath, Esther. *A Study in Social Treatment: The Approach to the Parent*. New York, The Commonwealth Fund, 1933. xviii+163 p.

Howard, Frank E. and Patry, Frederick L. *Mental Health*. New York, Harper and Brothers, 1935. xvi+551 p.

Isaacs, Susan. *Nursery Years*. New York, Vanguard Press, 1936. 138 p.

Jersild, A. T. *Child Psychology*. Revised and Enlarged. New York, Prentice-Hall, 1940. 592 p.

Keliher, Alice V. *Life and Growth*. New York, D. Appleton-Century Company, 1938. 245 p.

Levy, John and Munroe, Ruth. *The Happy Family*. New York, A. A. Knopf, 1938. 319 p.

Louttit, C. M. *Clinical Psychology*. New York, Harper and Brothers, 1936. xx+695 p.

Morgan, John J. B. *Psychology of the Unadjusted School Child*. Revised Edition. New York, The Macmillan Company, 1936. vii+339 p.

Mowrer, Ernest R. *The Family, Its Organization and Disorganization*. Chicago, University of Chicago Press, 1932. xi+364 p.

Munn, Norman L. *Psychological Development*. Boston, Houghton Mifflin Company, 1938. xx+582 p.

Plant, James S. *Personality and the Cultural Pattern.* New York, The Commonwealth Fund, 1937. x+432 p.

Rand, W., Sweeny, M. E., and Vincent, E. L. *Growth and Development of the Young Child.* Third Edition Revised. Philadelphia, W. B. Saunders Company, 1940. x+462 p.

Sait, Una M. *New Horizons for the Family.* New York, The Macmillan Company, 1938. xiii+772 p.

Sherman, Mandel. *Mental Conflicts and Personality.* New York, Longmans, Green and Company, 1938. viii+319 p.

Strain, Frances B. *New Patterns in Sex Teaching.* New York, D. Appleton-Century Company, 1934. xvi+241 p.

Strang, Ruth M. *An Introduction to Child Study.* Revised Edition. New York, The Macmillan Company, 1938. xv+681 p.

Witty, Paul A. and Skinner, Charles E. *Mental Hygiene in Modern Education.* New York, Farrar and Rinehart, 1939. x+539 p.